KINGSLEY AMIS

a reference guide

A
Reference
Publication
in
Literature

Ronald Gottesman
Editor

KINGSLEY AMIS

a reference guide

DALE SALWAK

G.K. HALL & CO.
70 LINCOLN STREET, BOSTON, MASS.

Library of Congress Cataloging in Publication Data
Salwak, Dale.
  Kingsley Amis.

  (A Reference publication in literature)
  Includes index.
  1. Amis, Kingsley — Bibliography. I. Series:
Reference publications in literature.
Z8032.52.S24   [PR6001.M6]   016.828'9'1409   78-4244
ISBN 0-8161-8062-8

This publication is printed on permanent/durable acid-free paper
MANUFACTURED IN THE UNITED STATES OF AMERICA

*For
my parents*

Contents

Introduction

Almost from the beginning of his career, Kingsley Amis has enjoyed the attention of numerous and influential commentators. Because his career is filled with innovations, surprises, and variations in techniques and themes, it is not surprising that until recently critics and reviewers alike have found it difficult to make a definitive statement about his achievements. The range of his work is extraordinary: fiction, poetry, reviews, criticism, humor, science fiction, and biography. But of all his writings, his novels seem to inspire the greatest amount of critical comment. This critical reception may be divided into four major areas of concern.

The first area covers those who treat the early works as "angry" novels of protest against the contemporary social, political, and economic scene in Britain. The themes they find include: (1) resentment of a rigid class stratification; (2) rejection of formal institutional ties and relationships; (3) discouragement with economic insecurities and low status of those without money; (4) loathing of pretentiousness in any form, and (5) disenchantment with the past. Because many of Amis' contemporaries, including John Wain, John Osborne, John Braine, and Alan Sillitoe, seem to express similar concerns, and because many came from working or lower-middle class backgrounds, went to Oxford or Cambridge, and taught for a time at a provincial university, journalists soon spoke of them as belonging to a literary movement. The "Angry Young Men," as their heroes were called, were educated men who didn't want to be gentlemen: "a new, rootless, faithless, classless class" lacking in manners and morals (1964.B4). W. Somerset Maugham called them "mean, malicious and envious...scum," and warned that these men would some day rule England (1955.B13). Moreover, critics even confused the characters with the writers themselves. For example, Amis' Jim Dixon (in Lucky Jim) was appalled by the tediousness and falseness of academic life; therefore, Dixon was interpreted as a symbol of anti-intellectualism. Dixon taught at a provincial university; therefore, he became a symbol of contempt for Cambridge and Oxford. And, Amis himself taught at a provincial university (Swansea); therefore, he and Dixon became one and the same in the minds of many critics. However, like all literary generalizations, this one, no sooner made, was modified for Kingsley Amis at least.

The second area of concern includes those writers who find it difficult to discuss Amis' fiction because it seems so artless. His
straightforward plotting, gift for characterization, and ability to
tell a good story, they say, are resistant to the modern techniques of
literary criticism. For example, because Amis lacks the obscurity,
complexity, and technical virtuosity of James Joyce or William
Faulkner, these critics suggest that he is not to be valued as highly.
This attitude actually reveals more about the tenets of much modern
criticism than it does about Amis. In many of the early reviews,
writers call Amis essentially a comic novelist, an entertainer, or an
amiable satirist not unlike P.G. Wodehouse, the Marx Brothers, or
Henry Fielding. Furthermore, his interests in the genres of the detective and ghost story, the James Bond thriller, and the science
fiction tale confirm for these critics that Amis is a writer of neither
depth nor serious intent.

Looking beyond the social commentary and entertainment, another
group finds a distinct relationship between Amis' novels and the "new
sincerity" of the so-called Movement poets of the 1950's and later.
These poets (including Philip Larkin, Amis, John Wain, and D.J. Enright,
all of whom also wrote fiction) saw their poetry as an alternative to
the symbolic and allusive poetry of T.S. Eliot and his followers. In
a movement away from allusion, obscurity, and excess of style, the
poets encouraged precision, lucidity, and craftsmanship. They concentrated on honesty of thought and feeling to emphasize a "businesslike
intention to communicate with the reader" (1970.B28). A number of
critics suggest that, like his poetry, Amis' deceptively simple novels
have been written with the same criteria he imposed on his poetry; thus,
they must be looked at carefully with a kind of standard applicable in
the nineteenth century. It will not work to read Amis with a measure
suitable only to Joyce or Faulkner. Rather, Amis' intellectual and
literary ancestors antedate the great modernist writers, and they have
helped to shape him into a kind of nineteenth century clergyman: a
literate man of good will who seeks to please and instruct people of
some intelligence. His novels may be appreciated for their common-
sensical approach. He writes clearly. He avoids extremes or excessive
stylistic experimentation. He is witty, satirical, and often didactic.

Fourthly, and more recently, critics look back over Amis' career
to find a consistent moral judgment quite visible beneath the social
commentary, entertainment, and traditional techniques. Beginning in
a world filled with verbal jokes, masquerades and incidents, Amis'
view of life grows increasingly pessimistic until he arrives at a
fearfully grim vision of a nightmare world filled with hostility, violence, sexual abuse, and self-destruction. A number of scholarly articles suggest that, by contrast, Amis stands for decency and common
sense and for treating people rightly and honestly. His novels emphasize the necessity of good works and of trying to live a moral life
in the natural--as opposed to the supernatural--world. Although this
moral seriousness is only hinted at in Lucky Jim, it becomes increasingly evident with Take A Girl Like You, his fourth novel. Whereas

in <u>Lucky Jim</u> the values are "hidden" beneath a comic narrative, now the comedy is submerged beneath a more serious treatment. Thus, <u>Take A Girl Like You</u> is a turning point for him in a number of ways. The characterization is more complex, the moral problems are more intense, and the point of view is not limited to only one central character. Moreover, the novel represents an increase in the pessimistic view of life and a decrease in the element of horseplay and high spirits.

In such later novels as <u>The Anti-Death League</u>, <u>The Green Man</u>, and <u>The Alteration</u>, Amis continues to see life more darkly as he shifts to an increasingly metaphysical, even theological concern. Now contemporary England is viewed as a wasteland of the spirit as his characters try vainly to cope with a precarious world filled with madness and hysteria. It is a world in which all of the traditional certainties—faith, love, loyalty, responsibility, decency—have lost their power to comfort and sustain. Man is left groping in the dark of a nightmare world.

Although Amis is first and foremost a novelist, his other literary activities have also received attention. It is largely because Amis is a respected novelist that critics have turned to his other writings for the insight they give into the man and his fiction. For example, scholars point out that his criticism and reviews are often motivated by a cultivated Philistinism. He dislikes anything which might be construed as literary affectation. He lacks political commitment. Moreover, he is a purveyor of segments of mass culture and a rationalist with a definite moral concern. These themes, which are expressed indirectly in the peripheral works, are explored in greater depth in his fiction.

Although no bibliography of this kind is ever complete, every attempt has been made to make as comprehensive a listing of the criticism as possible. I have included items for 1977 of which I am aware, but the entries for that year are understandably incomplete. The annotations are descriptive, not evaluative. In the few cases where I was unable to see the item cited, I have noted with an asterisk before the entry, and included in the annotation a note indicating the source of the work. In my abstracts of interviews, bibliographies, and biographical notes, I emphasize scope except in the case of very brief items. Thus, the central intention has been to present a reference guide that will help the scholar and other interested readers to trace Amis' growing and constantly changing literary reputation; hopefully, it will also help them to discover the various interpretations of his works.

This reference guide is arranged by date of publication of writings on Amis. Each year is divided into two sections. The first section, "A," lists full-length books and dissertations devoted exclusively to Amis. The second section, "B," lists all articles and reviews as well as books only partially devoted to Amis. Names of periodicals and newspapers are given as they appear on title pages of the issues in which the articles appeared. The works cited for any given year are listed alphabetically by author and are numbered according to their order of appearance in the "A" or "B" section. An article cited as "1973.B4" would be the fourth article in the "B" section for 1973. This code is employed within the text to refer to reprints and scholarly replies; it is also used in the index at the back of the guide. The index is inclusive, with authors, titles, and subjects interfiled.

I owe a great deal to many people: to Professor Stephen C. Moore at the University of Southern California, for his constructive criticism and other assistance; to Dr. Gordon N. Ray, President of the John Simon Guggenheim Memorial Foundation, who encouraged me and arranged for me to meet and interview Kingsley Amis; to Myrtle C. Bachelder at the University of Chicago, for financial assistance; to Professor L. David Sundstrand at Citrus College and my mother, Frances H. Salwak, for their detailed corrections and suggestions; and to Kingsley Amis, who treated me with the utmost generosity and whose correspondence with me proved invaluable.

I should also like to thank Dorothy Warriner and Lois Bond of the Hayden Memorial Library at Citrus College for their help in locating and obtaining material through inter-library loan. Lastly, this reference guide benefited greatly from J. Donn Vann and James T.F. Tanner's "Kingsley Amis: A Checklist of Recent Criticism" (1969.B45), from Rubin Rabinovitz' bibliography (1967.B28), and from Jack Benoit Gohn's <u>Kingsley Amis: A Checklist</u> (1967.A1). I have discovered several items not included by Gohn, corrected a number of minor errors in his list, and provided more detailed and comprehensive annotations.

Writings about Kingsley Amis,
1951-1977

1951 A BOOKS - NONE

1951 B SHORTER WRITINGS

    1   ANON. "Undergraduate Poetry." <u>The Times Literary Supplement</u>
        (13 April), p. 232.
           Review of <u>Oxford Poetry</u>. Finds in the poem "Backgrounds"
        a "hard use" of language with a barely perceptible "enforced
        local meaning."

1954 A BOOKS - NONE

1954 B SHORTER WRITINGS

    1   ALLEN, WALTER. "New Novels." <u>New Statesman and Nation</u>, 47
        (30 January), 136-137.
           Review of <u>Lucky Jim</u>. "A novelist of formidable and un-
        comfortable talent" whose comic novel reminds one of the
        best of the Marx Brothers films. Jim Dixon is a new hero:
        graceless, exasperated, and sensitive to phoniness. Re-
        printed: 1959.B1.

    2   ANON. "New Fiction: Standing Alone." London <u>Times</u> (27 Janu-
        ary), p. 8.
           Review of <u>Lucky Jim</u>. Calls Jim Dixon a "genuinely comic
        yet credible character" whom Amis shows both sympathetically
        and humorously. Dixon's integrity makes him likable. De-
        spite his difficulties, "it is surprising but pleasing to
        find that he has no chip on his shoulder but instead a mis-
        chievous imp whose irresistible impulses get him deeper and
        deeper into the mire of official disapproval." His standby
        and salvation is "a strong sense of humor that enables him
        to make light of much distress and disaster." Although the
        style is at times rough, Amis has a sharp eye for character.

    3   ANON. "Contemporary Portraits." <u>The Times Literary Supplement</u>
        (12 February), p. 101.

1954

    Review of <u>Lucky Jim</u>. Sees Jim Dixon as a typical sub-
hero appearing as protagonist in more and more postwar novels. As the classic little man, Dixon is "buffeted by life
and the victim of misfortune, but, through his education,
able to see quite clearly what's happening." The social
comedy is excellent.

4   ANON. "Fiction." <u>Booklist</u>, 50 (15 February), 239.
    Brief favorable mention of <u>Lucky Jim</u>. Calls the novel
"a good-natured caricature of the learned professions."
Jim Dixon is a kind of grown-up Peck's bad boy.

5   ANON. "Tradition and Originality." <u>The Times Literary Supple-
ment</u> (19 February), p. 122.
    Review of <u>A Frame of Mind</u>. Like John Wain, Amis repre-
sents a reaction against the neo-romanticism of the 1940's.
Finds an individual humor with a serious moral in the comic
poems. Amis frequently harks back to the styles of early
Auden.

6   ANON. "Fiction." <u>Kirkus</u>, 21 (15 November), 746.
    Review of <u>Lucky Jim</u>. "Absolute anglophiles may find this
gay and sportive but the average American reader could dis-
miss it as an arid intellectual exercise."

7   BETJEMAN, JOHN. "Amusing Story of Life at a Provincial University." London <u>Daily Telegraph</u> (5 February), p. 8.
    Review of <u>Lucky Jim</u>. Amis' "tolerant contempt" for aca-
demics is the novel's most amusing and refreshing feature.
The distinct characters, suspense, and happy ending contrib-
ute to "a Harold Lloyd film or a Buster Keaton film in
prose."

8   CHAPMAN, HESTER W. "New Novels." <u>Listener</u>, 51 (18 March), 495.
    Review of <u>Lucky Jim</u>. Although different in treatment,
outlook and style, Amis' technique is at exactly the same
point of development as Jane Lane's in <u>Thunder on St. Paul's
Day</u>. The novel is entertaining with some serious comment
beneath the surface. Jim Dixon is both a charmer and "the
butt, raconteur and battered yet cynically adaptable onlooker
found in the work of Dickens, Sterne and Swift."

9   CHAUCER, DAVID. "Book Reviews." <u>Shenandoah</u>, 6 (Winter), 81-83.
    Review of <u>Lucky Jim</u>. Calls this a satire on academic
life somewhat reminiscent of Evelyn Waugh. Amis' strengths
are "deft writing" and a gift for characterization, but his
real achievement is Jim Dixon, who reminds us that we know

at least one person like him. Notes that Dixon does not
become a fool.

10 DOBRÉE, BONAMY. "English Poetry Today: the Younger Generation." Sewanee Review, 62 (Autumn), 609-610.
    Labels Amis and his contemporaries "New University Wits."
Theirs is poetry of the intellect: a delightful exercise
when being written and an "act of kindness" when being read.

11 FULLER, EDMUND. "Academic Intrigues." New York Times Book
Review (31 January), p. 20.
    Review of Lucky Jim. Calls it a "clever, typically En-
glish" book. Some will find it highly amusing; others will
find it trivial. Reprinted: 1954.B14.

12 _____. "Briefly Noted: Fiction." New Yorker, 30 (6 March),
116.
    Review of Lucky Jim. Calls this an unusual first novel.
Amis displays "talent, humor, and human sympathy." He is
"direct, sensible, and often extremely funny."

13 _____. "Teacher's Misadventures." New York Herald Tribune
Book Review (25 April), p. 17.
    Reprint of 1954.B12.

14 HARTLEY, ANTHONY. "New Verse." Spectator, 192 (2 April), 411.
    Review of A Frame of Mind. The tone of many of these
poems calls to mind the satire of Lucky Jim. Amis has a
personality of his own here, for "the poems depend for their
effect on a delicate balance between self-assertion and self-
criticism."

15 HODGART, PATRICIA. "New Fiction." Manchester Guardian (2 February), p. 4.
    Review of Lucky Jim. As a misfit in academic life, Jim
Dixon is lazy and despicable like Evelyn Waugh's picaros,
but he triumphs in the end. The novel, however, lacks a
strong climax. Reprint: 1954.B17.

16 _____. "Some Recent Fiction." Manchester Guardian Weekly (11
February), p. 10.
    Reprint of 1954.B15.

17 McGIVERING, HELEN. "New Novels." Time & Tide, 35 (6 February),
185.
    Review of Lucky Jim. A very funny and highly intelligent
novel. "Mr. Amis writes with zest and enjoyment about the

1954

boredom and fury that his awful characters engender, and
his accurate observation of them makes them a splendid
entertainment."

18   METCALF, JOHN. "New Novels." Spectator, 192 (29 January),
132.
      Review of Lucky Jim. A very funny, very human novel fil-
led with acute observations by Amis. The happy ending is
not contrived, but comes about naturally. Jim Dixon is a
completely believable character. The only weakness is in a
tendency towards caricature in a couple of minor characters
and in the too early, too obvious appearance of the bene-
factor.

19   O'FAOLAIN, SEAN. "New Novels." Observer (24 January), p. 9.
      Lucky Jim is a rare novel because it is both "comic and
true." Amis' great achievement is "to have made the gayest
of bricks with the most common straw."

20   POORE, CHARLES. "Books of the Times." New York Times (27
July), p. 19.
      Review of Lucky Jim. "A brilliantly scatterbrained novel"
about a character who seems to have stepped out of a
Wodehouse novel into the world of Arnold Toynbee. The moral
is that a lot of learning, concentrated in a critical form,
is a disaster. Sees primarily "a ferocious struggle for
preferment and advancement, in a series of cheerfully irre-
sponsible vignettes."

21   POWELL, ANTHONY. "Booking Office." Punch, 226 (3 February),
188.
      Review of Lucky Jim. Amis is amusing and farcical with
an excellent sense of character. Although perhaps a shade
overwritten, the novel has "energy and form, and a real
power of presenting the academic world it describes."

22   SCOTT, GEORGE. "A bright first novel about a very bright man."
Truth, 154 (5 February), 185.
      Review of Lucky Jim. Unlike John Wain's Hurry On Down,
Amis' novel offers a more intense feel of the contemporary
scene and a more organic, less diffuse humor. Jim Dixon
relies more on luck than judgment; in him, many thousands of
postwar young men will see themselves. His jokes and invec-
tive remind one of Joyce Cary's Gulley Jimson. At the end
of the novel, Dixon is strong because he stops pretending to
be something he isn't and turns to his natural self.

23 SWAN, MICHAEL. "Book Reviews." <u>London Magazine</u>, OS 1 (April),
       88-90.
           Review of <u>Lucky Jim</u>. Like John Wain and Godfrey Smith,
       Amis presents the metropolitan and provincial point of view
       in action. As a genuinely comic novel, <u>Lucky Jim</u>'s source
       of satire is "indignation, anger, hatred," but Amis often
       comes near to destroying the situation with "prolixity."

24 WEBSTER, HARVEY CURTIS. "A Scholar's Quest." <u>Saturday Review</u>,
       37 (20 February), 20.
           Review of <u>Lucky Jim</u>. A good novel because the plot moves
       and keeps the reader guessing and because the Welch family
       is as real as Jim Dixon and Christine Callaghan. Amis writes
       without clichés or awkwardness, and "promises a lot more than
       he has yet fulfilled."

1955 A BOOKS - NONE

1955 B SHORTER WRITINGS

1   ANON. "Social Misfits." <u>The Times Literary Supplement</u> (16
       September), p. 537.
           Review of <u>That Uncertain Feeling</u>. One of the reasons for
       Amis' success is his deliberately irresponsible class-con-
       sciousness. Although a successful serio-comic novelist,
       however, he treats his characters too naturalistically.
       Amis fails to avoid sentiment in his treatment of the rela-
       tionship between the hero and his wife; as in the Marx
       Brothers films, both the insulter and the insulted must be
       treated without sentiment.

2   ANON. "Fiction." <u>Kirkus</u>, 23 (15 December), 895.
           Brief mention of <u>That Uncertain Feeling</u>.

3   BETJEMAN, JOHN. "Kingsley Amis's Second Novel is Wittier than
       his First." London <u>Daily Telegraph</u> (19 August), p. 8.
           Brief review of <u>That Uncertain Feeling</u>. Amis' comedy
       more controlled and funnier than it is in <u>Lucky Jim</u>.

4   BOSTOCK, ANNA. "Class Skirmish." <u>Manchester Guardian Weekly</u>
       (1 September), p. 101.
           Reprint of 1955.B5.

5   _____. "New Novels." <u>Manchester Guardian</u> (23 August), p. 4.
           Review of <u>That Uncertain Feeling</u>. This is not a novel
       of substance, but rather a "disgruntled novel" filled with

1955

        contempt. The last sentence is the key line to the book, for it reveals a bitter nostalgia. Reprinted: 1955.B4.

6   BOWEN, ELIZABETH. "An African Boyhood." Tatler, 217 (7 September), 416, 434.
        Brief review of That Uncertain Feeling. Discusses the novel's relation to Lucky Jim and to the so-called "Angry Young Men."

7   CORKE, HILARY. "Bad Conscience." Encounter, 5 (October), 87-88.
        Review of That Uncertain Feeling. A readable novel in which Amis plays down the farce. It is a "more solid and satisfactory affair" than Lucky Jim for it represents an "advance in consistency and balance." Praises the rational analysis of character, the satire and diction, but is disturbed by the negative attitude of Amis and narrator, for it is founded on obtuseness; that is, Amis is "anti-art, anti-knowledge, anti-tradition, anti-manners--opposed, in fact, on principle, to 'the best that is known or thought' or enjoyed or done."

8   DERRICK, CHRISTOPHER. "Anti-Heroides." Tablet, 206 (10 September), 256.
        Review of That Uncertain Feeling. Although similar to John Wain's Living in the Present (as a moral comedy on self-pity and adultery), Amis' comedy is happier, subtler and "naughtier" than Wain's. Amis is precise and objective in his satire. He has a sharp though affectionate eye for human nature.

9   FANE, VERNON. "A Song To Sing--O!" Sphere, 228 (1 October), 34.
        Review of That Uncertain Feeling. Amis creates great fun for the reader as he "manages to be both hilarious and sympathetic about a Welsh community without being in the slightest bit Welsh." Notes some unevenness resulting from passages where Amis is either too serious or not serious enough.

10   KALB, B. "Three Comers." Saturday Review, 38 (7 May), 22.
        Brief interview in which Amis dismisses any attempt to identify him with a particular school or with such writers as John Wain and Iris Murdoch. Includes some biographical data.

11   LANE, MARGARET. "New Fiction." London Sunday Times (21 August), p. 5.

Review of <u>That Uncertain Feeling</u>. Praises the convincing detail. By the end, Amis makes us feel a "tolerant
affection" for a man neither likable nor admirable. Though
unsentimental and funny, there is an undercurrent of "deadly
truth."

12 LISTER, RICHARD. "New Novels." <u>New Statesman and Nation</u>, 50
        (20 August), 222.
        Review of <u>That Uncertain Feeling</u>. Amis contrasts the
old world and the new in a mixture of disgust and farce.
He writes with a lack of refinement. The ending is unconvincing, his world is mean, and his values are non-existent.
Although he shows little feeling for his characters, he does
have a sharp eye for people's manners and dialogue.

13 MAUGHAM, SOMERSET. "Books of the Year--1." London <u>Sunday</u>
        <u>Times</u> (25 December), p. 4.
        Review of <u>Lucky Jim</u>. Although Amis is a talented, keen
observer, his hero is representative of a new group of characters who lack manners, don't go to the university to ac-
quire culture, and are unable to deal with social predicaments.
They are "mean, malicious, and envious....They are scum."
Says the cultural life of England is passing to a new class,
to those who have gone on to the university on their brains
regardless of their origins.

14 OAKES, PHILIP. "Recent fiction." <u>Truth</u>, 155 (26 August),
        1077-1078.
        Review of <u>That Uncertain Feeling</u>. As a funny, sympathetic,
and serious book, this is the "best, brightest and most
truthful book about a modern marriage to appear in many a
year." It marks an important advance for Amis as a mature
novelist. He is no longer just a comic writer. Praises the
lively and natural dialogue, the convincing characterization,
and the authentic sense of locale.

15 QUENNELL, PETER. "Bird Men ARE Just a Flight of Imagination."
        London <u>Daily Mail</u> (26 August), p. 6.
        Brief mention of <u>That Uncertain Feeling</u>. Also comments
on <u>Lucky Jim</u>.

16 QUIGLEY, ISABEL. "New Novels." <u>Spectator</u>, 195 (2 September),
        316-317.
        Review of <u>That Uncertain Feeling</u>. Amis takes a new di-
rection in this novel. His technique is advanced and
tighter, and he has expanded his world somewhat. Although
a good storyteller as he balances the reader's amusement

1955

and exasperation, the stock comedy scenes are contrived and tiresome.
Excerpted in 1966.B60.

17 RAYMOND, JOHN. "Portrait of the New Elizabethan." London News Chronicle (8 September), p. 8.
Brief mention of That Uncertain Feeling. In John Lewis we see another dimension to the Amis hero already established in Lucky Jim, for his moral problems are more intense.

18 SCOTT, J.D. "The British Novel: Lively As A Cricket." Saturday Review, 38 (7 May), 21-23, 46.
An examination of the contemporary English novel. Sees in Lucky Jim a classlessness reminiscent of William Cooper's Scenes from Provincial Life. Calls Lucky Jim "the most ludicrously funny work" since 1945.

19 TOYNBEE, PHILIP. "Class Comedy." Observer (21 August), p. 9.
Brief review of That Uncertain Feeling. As a member of the unprivileged class, John Lewis aspires to the better life, even if it means committing adultery. Thus, the novel focuses on the conflict between the privileged and unprivileged.

20 WRIGHT, DAVID. "Beginning with Amis." Time & Tide, 36 (27 August), 1114-1115.
Review of That Uncertain Feeling. Amis is to the 1950's what Aldous Huxley was to the 1920's. In this novel, the theme "is the dinginess of contemporary society, provincial culture, contemporary marriage, provincial adultery and contemporary wire-pulling." Notes that because John Lewis' code of conduct is vague, his believability diminishes when he turns down the job. Amis' wit is a bit too "donnish" at times. Certain comic asides, such as the references to Dylan Thomas and the masquerade in the Welsh costume, distract the reader.

1956 A BOOKS - NONE

1956 B SHORTER WRITINGS

1 ALVAREZ, A. "A Joke's a Joke." Observer (18 November), p. 11.
Brief review of A Case of Samples. Amis' poetry is witty and often satirical.

2 ANON. "Fiction." Booklist, 52 (15 April), 338.
Brief mention of That Uncertain Feeling. Calls it a

"diverting tale" of John Lewis' amours and other adventures. Notes that Lewis grows up a little by the end.

3   ANON. "Taking Aim." <u>The Times Literary Supplement</u> (7 December), p. 735.
        Review of <u>A Case of Samples</u>. Amis is being deadly earnest and does have a claim to be taken seriously. Sometimes his refusal to be taken in by certain postures becomes a posture. Finds a note of tenderness in "Nocturne."

4   BULLOCK, FLORENCE HAXTON. "Dalliance." <u>New York Herald Tribune Book Review</u> (26 February), p. 8.
        Review of <u>That Uncertain Feeling</u>. Amis' message "is that man is by nature promiscuous and that women—or at any rate wives—tend to resent it." An amusing and light novel, it "is at the same time a tender, knowing little book based on considerable shrewd insight into human nature and some skill in portraying it."

5   CARTER, THOMAS H. "Book Reviews." <u>Shenandoah</u>, 7 (Summer), 57-58.
        Review of <u>That Uncertain Feeling</u>. The tone is dominated by a seriousness hinted at in <u>Lucky Jim</u>. This tone makes the comedy more assured. Amis is a satirist who sees his characters clearly; the issues at stake are "human and moral."

6   CHASE, RICHARD. "Middlebrow England: the Novels of Kingsley Amis." <u>Commentary</u>, 22 (September), 263-269.
        As an undeclared leader of a new generation of English writers, Amis expresses an "Americanization" of English life and culture in <u>Lucky Jim</u> and <u>That Uncertain Feeling</u>. He uses comedy as a weapon of a newly rising class of the intellectual—the middlebrow. His style is reminiscent of some of the 1920's novels; his comedic talents remind one of Harold Lloyd. He is original, and readers find him both relevant and amusing because of his acute perception of the personal life. The "spectacle of life as it is being actually led" is more real and pressing than the life of ideas and of art. Amis' attitude is "a provincial, anti-intellectual, protestant moralism."

7   CONQUEST, ROBERT. "Poems and Poses." <u>Spectator</u>, 197 (23 November), 743.
        Review of <u>A Case of Samples</u>. Amis is a real poet, showing great feeling and intelligence. His theme is the human condition and men's attitudes to women. His style is clear, strong, sometimes light, but always serious in intent. This is a "technically brilliant" collection of poems.

1956

8 CORKE, HILARY. "Fear of the Best." New Statesman and Nation,
      52 (10 November), 599-600.
         Review of A Case of Samples. Amis is more of a versifier
      than a poet. This is honest, charming, light verse with a
      contemporary theme.

9 HOGAN, WILLIAM. Review of That Uncertain Feeling. San
      Francisco Chronicle (19 March), p. 27.
         Amis is a first-rate satirist who "packs his story with
      outlandish scenes of upper and middle-class English life
      while following the activities of this cast of generally
      unpleasant characters."

10 HYNES, SAM. "The 'Poor Sod' as Hero." Commonweal, 64 (13
      April), 51-53.
         Review of That Uncertain Feeling. Calls Amis a moralist
      who has to deal with an apparently amoral or immoral world.
      In this novel, "there is no certainty at all, except the
      certainty of feeling uncertain." John Lewis is representative
      of his time--"the rootless, valueless, anxious man."

11 LARKIN, PHILIP. "Separate Ways." Manchester Guardian (30 No-
      vember), p. 14.
         Review of A Case of Samples. Amis distinguishes himself
      with a combination of humor and seriousness. "Without it
      he seems dragged down by his own literal mindedness."

12 LEET, HERBERT L. "New Books Appraised: Fiction." Library
      Journal, 81 (1 February), 441.
         Brief mention of That Uncertain Feeling. Says Amis'
      humor is "aggravatingly coy and heavy-handed as he attempts
      to lighten John's caddish personality."

13 LINDSAY, JACK. "Regressions," in his After the Thirties: the
      Novel in Britain and Its Future. London: Lawrence and
      Wishart, p. 110.
         In a footnote, says Amis is a "post nihilist comedian."

14 OAKES, PHILIP. "A New Style in Heroes." The Observer (1 Jan-
      uary), p. 8.
         Assesses Amis' contribution to contemporary British
      fiction as he considers Jim Dixon (in Lucky Jim) and John
      Lewis (That Uncertain Feeling).

15 ROLO, CHARLES. "Reader's Choice: Fiction Roundup." The
      Atlantic Monthly, 197 (April), 87.
         Review of That Uncertain Feeling. This novel "represents

a new temper in British social comedy, which hitherto had
been rooted in an upper-class viewpoint." Notes an underlying
element of seriousness in the novel.

16   SIMPSON, LOUIS. "Fiction Chronicle." Hudson Review, 9 (Summer),
     304-305.
          Review of That Uncertain Feeling. Farce is Amis' weak-
     ness, for he throws real life away. Like Henry Fielding in
     Tom Jones, Amis reveals the self-deceptions of vanity in
     some truly comic scenes. John Lewis' central problem is
     familiar--"unlimited imagination, limited income."

17   SNOW, C.P. "Mr. Maugham and 'Lucky Jim.'" London Sunday Times
     (8 January), p. 6.
          A rebuttal of Maugham's attack against Lucky Jim (see
     1955.B13). Defends Amis by saying he has "invented a highly
     personal comic style," and that it is much more justifiable
     to see his characters as "present-day guardians of the puri-
     tan conscience." Concludes by saying that Amis' characters
     seem much like the men of 25 or 30 years ago, except that
     then men didn't consider themselves socially fixed.

18   STERN, JAMES. "Some Unpleasant People." New York Times Book
     Review (26 February), p. 4.
          Review of That Uncertain Feeling. The behavior of John
     Lewis, like Jim Dixon, is adolescent. His predicament is
     that he possesses an uncertain feeling for another man's
     wife and a dislike for culture and "the anglicized upper
     classes." While not convincing on Lewis' morality, Amis is
     convincing in his observations on seamy human nature, his
     grotesque imagery, his meticulous attention to detail, and
     the outlandish situations, all of which succeed in holding
     the reader's attention.

19   TINDALL, WILLIAM YORK. "Disenchantment," in his Forces in
     Modern British Literature: 1885-1956. New York: Vintage
     Books, pp. 107, 119.
          Lucky Jim, like some of Evelyn Waugh's novels, is a study
     of "academic incompetence." Amis' verse is clever, of the
     sort that T.E. Hulme esteemed.

20   WEBSTER, HARVEY CURTIS. "The Gay, Good-Bad People." Saturday
     Review, 39 (25 February), 17.
          Review of That Uncertain Feeling. Amis' latest novel fits
     into the tradition of the serio-comic British novel and is
     better than Lucky Jim. Notes that Amis likes the people he
     creates. John Lewis is "a poseur and hypocrite who sees
     through himself so clearly you can't help liking him." The

1957

other characters are good and bad people "who sometimes are
ridiculous, sometimes nearly novel, always trying to cope
with a society and an age that gives them genuine reasons
for anxiety."

21   WILSON, EDMUND. "Is It Possible to Pat Kingsley Amis?" The
      New Yorker, 32 (24 March), 140-147.
          Although Lucky Jim and That Uncertain Feeling fall into
      the tradition of Evelyn Waugh and Angus Wilson, Amis' novels
      differ in that we see everything from the point of view of
      baseless, unoriented young people. Comments on Amis' crit-
      ical reception and notes that for a number of reasons critics
      did not treat Amis' second novel as kindly as they did the
      first. Explains this by showing that whereas in Lucky Jim
      only the opponents are repulsive, in That Uncertain Feeling
      all of the characters are unpleasant. Moreover, the details
      in the second novel suggest a certain "coarseness" on the
      part of author and hero. Because it is told from the hero's
      point of view, we cannot escape his disgusting life, nor can
      we escape the feeling that Lewis' point of view is attrib-
      utable to Amis. These differences, together with the ob-
      servation that it is a more serious study, heavily influenced
      by American fiction in tone and dialogue, help account for
      its reception by critics. Reprinted: 1965.B60.

1957 A BOOKS - NONE

1957 B SHORTER WRITINGS

1   ANON. "Too Late The Mavericks." The Times Literary Supplement
     (8 March), p. 138.
         Review of Socialism and the intellectuals. Says this is
     a disappointing work. The prose is muddled, coarse, and
     vague, as are Amis' thoughts. Notes a relationship between
     the study and the anthology Mavericks.

2   ANON. "Classified Books: Literature." Booklist, 53 (15 April),
     422-423.
         Review of A Case of Samples. A diversity of poems in
     which Amis turns to "harsh expressions" in the interests of
     "honesty and immediacy."

3   ANON. "Books: Lucky Jim & His Pals." Time, 69 (27 May),
     106-108.
         Discusses Lucky Jim and Socialism and the Intellectuals
     and their relationship to the "Angry Young Men." Says
     Lucky Jim has become symbolic of "the small expectations and

raddled nerves of mid-twentieth century Britain--and especially its middle-class intellectuals--under the Welfare
State." As the most notable of the "Angry Young Men" works,
Lucky Jim marks the end of "the era of Utopian belief in
man's earthly salvation through socialism and sociology."
This is further expressed in Socialism and the Intellectuals,
the "first authentic manifesto of an apolitical literary
age." Amis advocates a retreat from politics. Of the group,
Amis is "its only conscientious craftsman and its only notable wit." Includes some biographical details.

4   ANON. "Science Fiction On The Third." London Times (7 Novem-
    ber), p. 3.
        Review of Touch and Go as it appeared on BBC's Third
    Programme. The struggle for survival is the situation here.
    Humans land on a planet devoid of human life, but with plants
    resentful of interference. However, the play is too short
    to locate the listener in a bizarre, unfamiliar environment.
    Although the action is exciting, the incidents tend to lose
    impact. Notes that this production coincidentally paralleled
    the launching of the Sputnik satellite.

5   BEAVAN, JOHN. "The New Intellectual." Spectator, 198 (11 Jan-
    uary), 38-39.
        Review of Socialism and the Intellectuals. Amis proposes
    that political writing in the 1930's "was a self-administered
    therapy for personal difficulties rather than a contribution
    to the reform of society." Beavan discounts this and says
    there is a correlation between the external conditions of
    the 1930's and the internal problems of Auden, Spender, and
    C. Day Lewis. Disagrees with Amis that the intellectual
    lives in a political void, or that he is a romantic in search
    of a cause. Sees a new era of political activity.

6   CRISPIN, EDMUND. "Unlucky Us." Observer (3 March), p. 15.
        Attempts to free Amis from the "Angry Young Man" label
    by noting that in three years, Lucky Jim has come to mean
    the opposite it did when first published. Says Amis has
    been confused with John Osborne, for which Amis has been the
    chief sufferer. Literary commentators need movements to
    write about, and in doing so "have sacrificed exactness to
    cross reference."

7   DOBRÉE, BONAMY. "No Man's Land." Sewanee Review, 65 (Spring),
    310, 313-315, 320-321.
        Attacks Lucky Jim as a farce whose central character suf-
    fers from a superficial inner conflict. There is no depth
    to the novel because Amis' criticism is jeering and rude,

1957

based on a complete failure to see his position in history, an inability to see any point of view other than his own, and "an exaggerated sense of class distinctions." Concludes that it is hard to tell what the book is trying to do.

8   ENGELBORGHS, MAURITS. "Nigel Dennis and Kingsley Amis." Dietsche Warrande en Belfort, 9 (Winter), 565-571.
        Discusses Lucky Jim and That Uncertain Feeling as they relate to the "Angry Young Men." Brief summary of the contents of both novels. (In Flemish.)

9   GREEN, MARTIN. "A Communication: Thoughts About Two Homes from Abroad." Partisan Review, 24 (Spring), 268.
        Unlike the heroes of American writers, who are generally supportive of American culture, Amis' heroes are in revolt against the dead culture of Britain, and "they see no way out in terms of spiritual or revolutionary elites." Both Jim Dixon and John Lewis find no real solution, for they are doomed to social defeat.

10 HOLLOWAY, JOHN. "Tank in the Stalls: Notes on the 'School of Anger.'" Hudson Review, 10 (Autumn), 424-429.
        Tries to relate the "Angry Young Men" to the tradition of the English novel by showing that Jim Dixon is not really a new kind of hero. His social aim is neutrality, and he is going back to nineteenth century preoccupations. Reprinted: 1959.B4; 1962.B14.

11 JOHNSON, PAUL. "Lucky Jim's Political Testament." New Statesman and Nation, 53 (12 January), 35-36.
        Review of Socialism and the Intellectuals. Although poorly written, this is an important and interesting tract. Amis claims to speak on behalf of the new Welfare State intellectuals, but fails to define "intellectual." Disagrees with Amis' premise by saying that self-interest is a necessary ingredient in politics; the intellectual is not disinterested. Concludes that this tract is out of date; it is, in fact, Jim Dixon's last will and testament.

12 KIZER, C. "Four English Poets." Poetry, 91 (October), 49-50.
        Review of A Case of Samples. Amis is surely not serious in this collection, for he stays away from exploration of his subjects in depth. In "Lessons," Amis displays a mock cynicism. Amis expresses many dislikes in these poems, most of which are boring.

13 McDONALD, GERALD D. "New Books Appraised: Poetry." Library Journal, 82 (1 May), 1248.

14

Review of A Case of Samples. Amis' poetry is "serious, weightily intellectual at times, but his wit and love of fun come breaking through."

14   MASSINGHAM, HUGH. "British Intellectuals on Strike." New Republic, 136 (4 March), 10-11.
Review of Socialism and the Intellectuals. Observes that this tract reveals that Amis and his coterie of intellectuals are bored by the British Labour Party, politics, and the Welfare State. These new writers are urged on by resentment and are distinguished from intellectuals of the past and from their immediate predecessors by their "provincialism."

15   MERWIN, W.S. "He Can Be Funny, Too." New York Times Book Review (17 March), p. 33.
Review of A Case of Samples. Discusses three kinds of poems in this collection: those "of generalized intellectual statement" somewhat reminiscent of William Empson; those serious poems, ironic or elegiac, or both; and those "overtly funny pieces," similar to Auden and Betjeman.

16   MILLGATE, MICHAEL. "A Communication: A Good Word for England." Partisan Review, 24 (Summer), 431.
In novels by Amis, Iris Murdoch, John Wain, in poems by Philip Larkin, Elizabeth Jennings, and Thom Gunn, and in plays by John Osborne, "one can discern at least the beginnings of a new and more hopeful movement--a movement toward honesty and away from hypocrisy, a reaction against political lies and social shams, a rejection of all cults of the gentleman." Eventually, we will see that this movement is in tune with E.M. Forster in his insistence on "honesty" and "naturalness" in human relationships.

17   _____. "An Uncertain Feeling in England." New Republic, 137 (9 September), 16-17.
Lucky Jim is the central work in a current mood of dissatisfaction represented in Look Back in Anger. Sees Jim Dixon as a "less violent version" of Jimmy Porter. Dixon is a type or symbol "of the socially disruptive hero for whom everything turns out well at the end." What is new to the English novel is the area of society he comes from.

18   PRITCHETT, V.S. "These Writers Couldn't Care Less." New York Times Book Review (28 April), pp. 1, 38-39.
Notes that the "Angry Young Men's" writings are marked by self, not society; that is, theirs is a switch from "idealism" to self-interest in the English novel. The

15

1957

authors represent a new class of "uprooted people." They
write in a "talking style, a debunking style." Many of
their novels are picaresque.

19   PROCTOR, MORTIMER R.   "The Cult of Oxford," in The English
University Novel. Berkeley and Los Angeles: University of
California Press, pp. 175-176.
     In Lucky Jim and That Uncertain Feeling, Amis' focus
upon the shams of academic life is "clear, merciless, and
very funny."

20   ROBINSON, ROBERT. "Radio." London Sunday Times (10 November),
p. 23.
     Review of Touch and Go on the BBC's Third Programme.
While Amis was inventive, science fiction must be more than
that; it must be imaginative. The sound effects were good,
but the actors' accents sounded phony. "Sounded like a goon
show without the humour."

21   SCOTT, J.D. "Britain's Angry Men." Saturday Review, 40 (27
July), 8-11.
     Explores and seeks to understand the origins of the myth-
ical "Angry Young Men." Says the attention given Amis and
others is not based on an accurate understanding of the novels, but rather on a reaction by class conscious England to
characters like Jim Dixon. Commentators point out that like
Jimmy Porter in Look Back in Anger, Dixon is representative
of a provincial point of view. He is ignorant of "Higher
Things," without culture, and unromantic.
     Actually, Dixon is a likable character who tries to be
himself and suffers. Simply, Dixon is an educated man who
doesn't want to be a gentleman, and this collective attitude
represents a change going on in England. This is the myth
of the "Angry Young Men."

22   SPENDER, STEPHEN. "Notes From A Diary." Encounter, 8 (March),
69-71.
     Review of Socialism and the Intellectuals. Praises Amis'
remarks about the 1930's as the most just he had read.
Amis' tone is "reluctant, rather warm-hearted, ultimately
willing...flirtation." Notes a dramatic relationship between writer and reader.

23   TOYNBEE, PHILIP. "The Politics of Lucky Jim." The Observer
(13 January), p. 11.
     In Socialism and the Intellectuals, Amis confuses "the
romantic and the moral motives in politics." This book was
written by "the fortunate, good-hearted, realistic, cunning

yet clumsy clown" we see in <u>Lucky Jim</u>, not by the "sour and iconoclastic rebel, moved principally by social envy and personal spite," that some readers have tried to make him.

24   WAIN, JOHN. "English Poetry: the Immediate Situation." <u>Sewanee Review</u>, 65 (Summer), 359-361.
        Categorizes Amis' poetry by illustrating there are no great resemblances between Amis and Philip Larkin or Donald Davie.

25   _____. "How It Strikes A Contemporary." <u>The Twentieth Century</u>, 161 (March), 234.
        Notes that <u>Lucky Jim</u> was distorted by critics with the intrusion of the class issue. Mentions that critics felt this novel established the persona for 1950's novels.

26   WATERMAN, ROLLENE. "Gallery of Lucky Jims." <u>Saturday Review</u>, 40 (27 July), 9.
        Brief biographical entry.

<u>1958 A BOOKS - NONE</u>

<u>1958 B SHORTER WRITINGS</u>

1   ALLEN, WALTER. "The Comic Trials of Being Abroad." <u>New York Herald Tribune Book Review</u> (9 March), p. 12.
        Review of <u>I Like It Here</u>. This is a disappointing book because Garnet Bowen is a "pale carbon" of Jim Dixon and John Lewis and because the shams Amis detects are not new.

2   ALPERT, HOLLIS. "Art of Bungling." <u>Saturday Review</u>, 41 (8 March), 17.
        Review of <u>I Like It Here</u>. Although witty, there is not much of a story to this novel, unlike Amis' first two novels. Identifies a serious undertone when he says the hero "looks not to be imprisoned in his unsatisfactory way of life, and...is going to muddle through somehow."

3   ALVAREZ, A. "Poetry of the 'Fifties: In England," in <u>International Literary Annual 1</u>. Edited by John Wain. London: John Calder, pp. 97, 102.
        As a poet, Amis shows common sense and restores the status of the poet.

4   ANON. "Taking It Easy." <u>The Times Literary Supplement</u> (17 January), p. 30.
        Review of <u>I Like It Here</u>. As a stand-in for Amis' own

1958

views, Garnet Bowen is seen in an ironical, self-deprecating way. A disappointing third novel.

5   ANON. "Portrait Gallery." London Sunday Times (26 January), p. 5.
    Brief interview in which Amis admits he never thought Lucky Jim would sell well. His response to the "Angry Young Man" controversy is cool. He agrees with the reviews of I Like It Here, but laughed a lot. Includes some biographical details.

6   ANON. "In the Thurber Manner." Newsweek, 51 (17 February), 111.
    Review of I Like It Here. Amis' work suggests the short stories of Thurber; his style, too, is more American than English. Concludes that his latest novel is "sophisticated, relentlessly comic, and to the American taste."

7   ANON. "Fiction." Booklist, 54 (1 March), 390.
    Review of I Like It Here. Garnet Bowen's difficulties are viewed by a detached novelist. Although the characters are cardboard, the satire is good and the humor is sophisticated.

8   ANON. "Briefly Noted." New Yorker, 34 (24 May), 150.
    Review of I Like It Here. The moral is that "married men who make a virtue of their incompetence in daily matters and chance encounters must go away from home if they want the laughter they provoke to remain kindly, musical, and pleasant to hear."

9   BAILHACHE, JEAN. "Angry Young Men." Les Langues Modernes (March-April), 31-46, also numbered 143-158.
    Discusses Amis' first three novels in context of the "Angry Young Man" myth and Amis' contemporaries. (In French.)

10   BODE, CARL. "Mr. Amis in Portugal." New York Times Book Review (23 February), p. 40.
    Review of I Like It Here. As an attempted combination travelogue and novel, this is a disappointing book with a slender plot and stock characters.

11   BREWER, D.S. "Proteus." Studies in English Literature. 72 (Summer), 58.
    Mentions Lucky Jim and That Uncertain Feeling in a brief assessment of the postwar novel in Britain.

12 BRINNIN, JOHN MALCOLM. "Young But Not Angry." <u>Mademoiselle</u>,
    46 (April), 150-151, 169-172.
        The term "Angry Young Man" is passé. It is only margin-
    ally related to Amis' novels and doesn't begin to define his
    poetry. Rather, Amis' poetry elicits little if any anger.
    He doesn't preach, he avoids the emotion of Dylan Thomas,
    and he, like the other Movement and Maverick poets, respects
    Philip Larkin as the voice of the group.

13 COLBY, WINETTA. "Kingsley Amis." <u>Wilson Library Bulletin</u>, 32
    (May), 618.
        Biographical background.

14 COUGHLAND, ROBERT. "Why Britain's Angry Young Men Boil Over:
    Most Talked About Writers of To-Day Reflect Frustration of
    Declining England." <u>Life</u>, 44 (26 May), 138-150.
        Brief summary of who the "Angry Young Men" are and what
    they write about. Not to be confused with the Beat genera-
    tion in the United States.

15 ESTY, WILLIAM. "A Failure of Invention." <u>New Republic</u>, 138
    (24 March), 21-22.
        Review of <u>I Like It Here</u>. Discusses the Amis hero to
    show that Garnet Bowen is a failure of invention. He is a
    bore, he is disappointing, and he works too hard to be an
    Amis hero. There is little fun in this novel. The games
    and anti-heroic self-depreciation seem gratuitous. Con-
    cludes that Amis needs a new hero figure or "an unembar-
    rassed grip on the old one."

16 FANE, VERNON. "A South American Childhood." <u>Sphere</u>, 232 (8
    January), 124.
        Review of <u>I Like It Here</u>. Amis is concerned with "the
    problem of men and women and households, but often inspired
    by a kind of explosive funniness and none the less profound
    for being expressed in many instances through positively
    flippant conversations." Passages in which Garnet Bowen
    communes with himself are reminiscent of the funny scenes
    in <u>Lucky Jim</u>. One improvement is that some of the characters
    "are quite prepossessing, whether physically or by their
    natures."

17 FIEDLER, LESLIE. "The Un-Angry Young Men: America's Post-War
    Generation." <u>Encounter</u>, 10 (January), 5, 10.
        Sees the image of a new age in <u>Lucky Jim</u> as comparable to
    Salinger's writings in the United States. Amis projects his
    dilemmas in <u>Lucky Jim</u>. Concludes that Amis is not well-
    informed in certain aspects of American literature.

1958

18   FRASER, GEORGE S. "New Novels." New Statesman, 55 (18 Janu-
     ary), 78.
          Review of I Like It Here. This is not a novel, but mere-
     ly a collection of impressions of Portugal. The plot, a
     variation of Anthony Powell's What's Become of Waring?,
     throws no light on character and only gets in the way.
     Notes that Amis leans more heavily on dialogue in this novel,
     and that it is hard to tell whether he approves or disap-
     proves of his characters. Garnet Bowen "could have been an
     alarming study in comic pliability."

19   FULLER, ROY. Review of I Like It Here. London Magazine, OS 5
     (February), 67-69.
          An occasionally lively, funny novel, obviously off the
     top of Amis' head. Unlike Lucky Jim--where he finds a
     "potential moral purpose, and intellectual force and deeper
     feeling"--there is no evidence of exploration of his powers
     here. Excerpted in 1966.B60.

20   GIBSON, WALKER. "You Mustn't Say Things Like That." Nation,
     187 (20 November), 410-411.
          Amis effectively attacks clichés and abuse of language
     in Lucky Jim. This is one reason the novel has received
     favorable reception among intellectuals.

21   GINDIN, JAMES. "The Reassertion of the Personal." Texas
     Quarterly, 4 (Fall), 126-134.
          In his first two novels, Amis returns to the tradition
     of British comedy, but with some differences. Unlike many
     comic novels of a generation ago, Lucky Jim ends happily
     but only after the hero proves his right to the prize. Amis
     is much more directly involved in the world as he finds it,
     and constructs his novels to provide "the widest possible
     opportunity for a direct and personal assertion in the midst
     of his own world." Comedy exaggerates, reforms, and criti-
     cizes to advocate the reasonable in social behavior and to
     promote the value and dignity of the individual, thereby
     avoiding sentimentality.

22   GREEN, MARTIN. "Amis and Salinger: the Latitude of Private
     Conscience." Chicago Review, 11 (Winter), 20-25.
          Both Amis and Salinger present a positive alternative
     not found in Hemingway, Greene, Faulkner, and others. Both
     play with words, present characters who fight against a
     world dominated by phonies, and personally involve them-
     selves in their writing. Their heroes are puritanical,
     even pedagogical, and concerned with the same problem: how

to find a place in a privileged society which to them is inadequate, even dangerous. There is an intimate relationship between reader and writer because both authors, in the end, are writing about the reader's problems.

23 HARKNESS, BRUCE. "The Lucky Crowd--Contemporary British Fiction." The English Journal, 47 (October), 387-397.
Examines Amis' first three novels in an attempt to define the new "school" of novelists' strengths and weaknesses.

24 HARVEY, W.T. "Have You Anything to Declare? or, Angry Young Men: Facts and Fiction," in International Literary Annual 1. Edited by John Wain. London: John Calder, pp. 56-57.
In That Uncertain Feeling, he sees Amis as a potentially serious writer. The novel is more realistic than Lucky Jim, it has a new moral complexity, and the characters have more dimensions. However, farce disrupts the novel, and the final chapter is superfluous.

25 HENDERSON, ROBERT W. "New Books Appraised; Fiction." Library Journal, 83 (15 February), 604.
Unfavorable mention of I Like It Here. Says the humor is adolescent and dull. The moral seriousness element that may be in the earlier novels is not readily discernible in this novel.

26 HILTON, FRANK. "Britain's New Class." Encore, 10 (February), 59-63.
Sees Jim Dixon as a "déclassed intelligent underdog" and as a character with whom people identify or would like to identify. He is, indeed, representative of a "new class" in Britain.

27 HOBSON, HAROLD. "As Read in London." Christian Science Monitor (16 January), p. 11.
Review of I Like It Here. It is obvious that Amis dislikes abroad and foreigners, for Garnet Bowen's troubles have a deep personal ring. The novel may diminish Amis' standing as a "socially committed satirist," but it will help establish him as "a satirist of independent views."

28 HOGAN, WILLIAM. Review of I Like It Here. San Francisco Chronicle (13 February), p. 35.
The obscure jokes are irritating, "especially when the jokes are Britishisms of the most untranslatable sort." Hardly a funny novel.

1958

29   HOUGH, GRAHAM. "Novels and Literary Commodities." <u>Encounter</u>,
         10 (March), 87.
              Review of <u>I Like It Here</u>. The plot serves mainly as a
         mechanism for "hanging chips on shoulders." Amis seems "to
         be the victim of an unfortunate obsession; he hates all this
         culture but he can't keep off it." Argues that Amis should
         seek psychiatric advice so that "he might either be able to
         keep away from the stuff altogether, or learn to live with
         his addiction and actually enjoy it."

30   HURRELL, JOHN D. "Class and Conscience in John Braine and
         Kingsley Amis." <u>Critique</u>, 2 (Spring-Summer), 39-53.
              Discusses the moral basis of Amis' comedy. Seeks to cor-
         rect the idea that Amis is an "Angry Young Man" by showing
         that Amis is a satirical novelist whose characters are caught
         in a conflict between the phony and the real, between a com-
         promise for security and integrity. Of the three novels
         <u>Lucky Jim</u> is consistent satire with Amis sufficiently de-
         tached from the character. Jim Dixon really wants to be
         dismissed, for then he would not be forced to compromise
         his values. Thus, Dixon is engaged in a pursuit of integ-
         rity. Contrary to reviews, <u>That Uncertain Feeling</u> is not an
         advance on <u>Lucky Jim</u>, for much of the humor is irrelevant,
         and the major scenes are almost totally serious. <u>I Like It
         Here</u> is the least controlled; the writing is careless, the
         attitude towards Bowen is ambivalent, and the satire is
         inconsistent.

31   HYNES, SAM. "Random Events and Random Characters." <u>Commonweal</u>,
         67 (21 March), 642-643.
              Review of <u>I Like It Here</u>. A disappointing novel because
         it is merely a series of farcical incidents tied to a trav-
         el narrative. It is marred by random events, random char-
         acters, and uncontrolled satire. Garnet Bowen's character
         is carelessly developed; his reactions are miscellaneous
         and not unified.

32   LEBOWITZ, NAOMI. "Kingsley Amis: the Penitent Hero."
         <u>Perspective</u>, 10 (Summer-Autumn), 129-136.
              Amis' first three novels are concerned with the problem
         of identity. Each character masquerades (on both aesthetic
         and ethical levels) and moves towards responsibility, only
         to be "redeemed through the realization that the man is more
         important than the actor." This is "the classical penitent
         returning to moral balance."

33   LESSING, DORIS. "The Small Personal Voice," in <u>Declaration</u>.
         Edited by Tom Maschler. London: MacGibbon and Kee, p. 199.

Disputes Amis' attitude in <u>Socialism and the Intellec-</u>
<u>tuals</u>, saying that Amis is generalizing from a mood of
disillusion.

34   MASCHLER, TOM, ed. "Introduction," in <u>Declaration</u>. Edited by
       Tom Maschler. London: MacGibbon and Kee, pp. 8-9.
          Comments on Amis' refusal to contribute to <u>Declaration</u>.
       Includes a quote from Amis' letter.

35   MILNE, ANGELA. "The Lucky Touch of Success." <u>Sketch</u>, 228
       (29 January), 126.
          Brief mention of <u>I Like It Here</u>.

36   NEMEROV, HOWARD. "Younger Poets: The Lyric Difficulty."
       <u>Kenyon Review</u>, 20 (Winter), 32.
          Review of <u>A Case of Samples</u>. Focuses on Amis' honesty
       in "Ode to the E-N-E-by-E Wind." "It is as though he had
       decided that the world exists only as literature, that he
       and his readers are too wise to be fooled any longer by so
       much literature, and that, in consequence, the remaining
       job for poetry...is to be more or less benevolently amused
       at itself and its former pretension." Excerpted: 1963.B23.
       Reprinted: 1963.B23.

37   QUINTON, ANTHONY, et al. "The New Novelists: An Enquiry."
       <u>London Magazine</u>, OS 5 (November), 13-17.
          <u>Lucky Jim</u> is brilliant for its comment on the British
       social environment, its "para-Lawrentian personalism," and
       its originality and verbal skill.

38   RAVEN, SIMON. "The Kingsley Amis Story." <u>The Spectator</u>, 200
       (17 January), 79.
          Notes that Amis' first three novels have the same essen-
       tial hero. He is wholesome and athletic, he distrusts
       culture, and his attitude is directed by a "puritanical
       artisan background." Unlike the first two novels, <u>I Like</u>
       <u>It Here</u> is loose in structure and is inconsistent. Although
       an indifferent book, it is a necessary stage in the devel-
       opment of the "Amis-figure."

39   ROLO, CHARLES. "Reader's Choice." <u>Atlantic Monthly</u>, 201
       (April), 88-89.
          Review of <u>I Like It Here</u>. A combination of the insular
       innocent abroad theme with a variant of <u>The Aspern Papers</u>
       plot. Amis mixes travel impressions and literary detective
       work to give the novel "something of a split personality."
       The satire lapses into "complacency and laziness." Garnet

1958

     Bowen is like a ventriloquist's dummy, mouthing Amis' pet peeves.

40   SHEBS, R.L. Review of I Like It Here. Chicago Sun Tribune (2 March), p. 8.
     The main strength is Amis' portrayal of manners. The dialogue is "pert and contemporary." Likes the cleverness, parody, and jest, but especially praises the characterization and ideas in the last three chapters.

41   SHRAPNEL, NORMAN. "Spender Hero and Amis Hero." Manchester Guardian (4 February), p. 4.
     Review of I Like It Here. A "slipshod work," an amusing "triviality." Reprinted: 1958.B42

42   _____. "Spender Hero and Amis Hero." Manchester Guardian Weekly (6 February), p. 10.
     Reprint of 1958.B41.

43   SPAIN, NANCY. "Mr. Ulysses Does It Again." London Daily Express (18 January), p. 4.
     Brief review of I Like It Here. More a travelogue than it is a novel, still Amis continues to treat his aversion to affectation with humor.

44   SPENDER, STEPHEN. "Anglo-Saxon Attitudes." Partisan Review, 25 (Winter), 112-113.
     Despite his "anti-culture pronouncements," Amis is a true academic.

45   _____. "When the Angry Men Grow Older." New York Times Book Review (20 July), pp. 1, 12.
     Says the "Angry Young Men" are "opposed to gentility and to the other cliquish standards of the older universities and the literary columns of the London weeklies." They attack the 1930's as unrealistic, naive, and snobbish. Concludes that the group will probably continue their protest when their anger is spent.

46   STANFORD, DEREK. "Beatniks and Angry Young Men." Meanjin, 17 (Summer), 413.
     Unlike the Beat poets, Amis' poetry is "ironical, oblique, and sardonic." It is "a poetry of criticism rather than of passion."

47   TOYNBEE, PHILIP. "Not So Lucky." The Observer (12 January), 14.
     Review of I Like It Here. "This writer's cloacal

tendencies have here got quite out of control." The novel
fails because Amis, as successor to P.G. Wodehouse, "has
not been aware of his true kinship and has mistaken the
nature of his talents."

48 WEAVER, ROBERT. "England's Angry Young Men--Mystics, Provin-
cials and Radicals." Queen's Quarterly, 65 (Summer),
189-191.
      Focuses on Amis as a comic novelist, provincial and phi-
listine. Notes a laziness in the first two novels that becomes more pronounced in I Like It Here. The problem with
Lucky Jim is that the reader doesn't always get the joke.

49 WRIGHT, DAVID. "Lucky Jim Abroad." Time & Tide, 39 (18 January), 75-76.
      Review of I Like It Here. Amis "extends his original
thesis of the boringness of monuments of literature to include practically every manifestation of European culture."
The Bowen family is archetypic British. The jokes wear a
little thin by the end. The information about Portugal is
tied together with a tenuous plot about establishing the
identity of a novelist.

1959 A BOOKS - NONE

1959 B SHORTER WRITINGS

1 ALLEN, WALTER. Review of Lucky Jim, in Beat Generation and
the Angry Young Men. Edited by Gene Feldman and Max
Gartenberg. New York: Citadel, pp. 339-340.
      Reprint of 1954.B1.

2 BALAKIAN, NONA. "The Flight from Innocence: England's Newest
Literary Generation." Books Abroad, 33 (Summer), 261-270.
      Defends Amis and his contemporaries against charges of
triviality and escapism by identifying his place in the
stream of the English novel and his departures from certain
established literary traditions. In Socialism and the Intellectuals, Amis reveals an intellectual honesty that is
carried over into his fiction. In Lucky Jim, beneath the
comedy, there is a harsh truth: Jim Dixon has to compro-
mise his better self in his search for status. That Uncertain Feeling is notable for its parody of romantic love
and its social comment. Amis brings to the English novel
"new ideas, a new style, and a new sense of the tragi-comic
essence of life."

1959

3   BODE, CARL. "The Redbrick Cinderellas." <u>College English</u>, 20
    (April), 331-337.
        Finds that <u>Lucky Jim</u> and <u>That Uncertain Feeling</u> are
    Cinderella stories with a male Cinderella, but by the time
    Amis reaches <u>I Like It Here</u>, he has worn himself out with
    the same type of hero.

4   FELDMAN, GENE AND MAX GARTENBERG, eds. <u>Beat Generation and
    the Angry Young Men</u>. New York: Citadel, pp. 14-17, 364-372.
        Compares and contrasts the "Angry Young Men" to the Beat
    generation as a social phenomenon. Includes reprint of
    1957.B10. Reprinted: 1962.B14.

5   GREEN, MARTIN. "British Decency." <u>Kenyon Review</u>, 21 (Fall),
    530-532.
        Discusses Amis' great achievement: the creation of the
    lower, middle-class, "non-gentlemanly conscience." His
    gift for detail enables him to distinguish between the gen-
    tleman and the decent man. The decent man evinces a puritan
    morality, a suspicion of all phoniness, an unheroic posture,
    and a strong moral sense of humor. Reprinted: 1960.B21.

6   JOHNSON, PAMELA HANSFORD. "Modern Fiction and the English
    Understatement." <u>The Times Literary Supplement</u> (7 August),
    p. iii.
        Says the new modern writers are rebelling against under-
    statement as a national characteristic in fiction. Amis and
    John Osborne "are wholly concerned with what is bad, or what
    seems bad to them, in the national life and are as noisy
    about that as Kipling was about the glories of the Empire."

7   KROLL, MORTON. "The Politics of Britain's Angry Young Men."
    <u>Western Political Quarterly</u>, 12 (June), 555-557.
        Jim Dixon is a hero repelled by a society it is hopeless
    to try to relate to. Amis, like the other "Angries," is
    for education, animalism, individualism, and social criti-
    cism, and is against class stratification, institutional
    ties, economic insecurity, disenchantment with the past, and
    things that will inhibit individual development. Although
    the writers are apolitical, Kroll notes "a strain of modern
    liberalism."

8   ROSS, T.J. "Books and Comment: The Curse of Refinement."
    <u>New Republic</u>, 140 (5 January), 18-20.
        In Amis, the creative act is aggressive, reaching the
    highest echelons of the educational system. Finds a hostil-
    ity to the "mandarin aesthetic" of the Eliot era in <u>I Like
    It Here</u>.

9   VAN DER VEEN, ADRIAAN. "Boze Jongelieden in een Zich Vernie-
     uende Engeland." <u>Vlaamse Gids</u>, 43 (April), 232-236.
          In his novels, Amis is disillusioned with the Welfare
     State and scornful of the aristocracy. Dicusses similar-
     ities between Amis and John Wain, John Braine, and John
     Osborne, and briefly mentions <u>Declaration</u>. (In Flemish.)

10   WEIMANN, ROBERT. "Die Literatur der <u>Angry Young Men</u>. Ein
     Beitrag zur Deutung englischer Gegenwartsliteratur."
     <u>Zeitschrift Fuer Anglistik und Amerikanistik</u>, 7 (January),
     117-189, passim.
          In a detailed study of the "Angry Young Men," the writers
     and their works, takes a Marxist approach. (In German.)

11   WILSON, COLIN. "The Writer and Publicity." <u>Encounter</u>, 13
     (November), 8-13.
          Examines Amis' public reputation, asserting that before
     television and gossip columns took an interest in writers,
     "personality only mattered in so far as it emerged in a
     writer's books." With the success of <u>Lucky Jim</u>, Amis "in-
     sisted on remaining the slightly aloof 'funny man,' puzzled
     by his own success." His next two novels received, respec-
     tively, polite and hostile reception, and so Amis is still
     the writer of <u>Lucky Jim</u> and nothing else.

<u>1960 A BOOKS - NONE</u>

<u>1960 B SHORTER WRITINGS</u>

1   ALLEN, WALTER. "That Uncertain Feeling." <u>New Statesman</u>, 60
     (24 September), 445.
          Review of <u>Take A Girl Like You</u>. Discusses the moral
     seriousness of the novel. Patrick Standish is a well-devel-
     oped character who, in a constant state of exasperation, is
     always testing himself. Jenny Bunn is a weak, conventional,
     scarcely differentiated character. Because she isn't treated
     satirically, "she appears less a young woman than a generous
     man's idea of a young woman."

2   ANON. Review of <u>New Maps of Hell</u>. <u>Kirkus</u>, 28 (1 January), 43.
          Brief mention of the study as a discourse on both science
     fiction and literary criticism.

3   ANON. "The Science Fiction Situation." <u>Time</u>, 75 (21 March),
     102.
          Review of <u>New Maps of Hell</u>. As a science fiction addict,
     Amis "speaks with dignity in behalf of his fellow incurables."

1960

4   ANON. "Briefly Noted." <u>New Yorker</u>, 36 (26 March), 163-164.
         Review of <u>New Maps of Hell</u>. An entertaining and percep-
      tive book in which Amis focuses on the themes and preoccu-
      pations of science fiction, noting a bold criticism of
      contemporary society.

5   ANON. "Classified Books: Literature." <u>Booklist</u> (15 May),
      p. 564.
         Brief mention of <u>New Maps of Hell</u>. Distinguished by a
      "keen wit" and critical judgment.

6   ANON. "Notes on Current Books." <u>Virginia Quarterly Review</u>,
      36 (Summer), xcii-xciii.
         Review of <u>New Maps of Hell</u>. An entertaining and illumi-
      nating work in which Amis covers the social and political
      situations in science fiction. Includes the evolution of
      science fiction writing.

7   ANON. "The Uses of Comic Vision: A Concealed Social Point in
      Playing for Laughs." <u>The Times Literary Supplement</u> (9 Sep-
      tember), p. ix.
         Discusses the social aspects of Amis' first three novels.
      <u>Lucky Jim</u> is about the preservation of one's integrity, and
      exemplifies England's insularity of humor and intense con-
      cern with class. In the next two novels, Amis is much more
      amiable and less serious. After <u>Lucky Jim</u> appeared, some
      critics said that the novel was "a vehicle for showing up
      the frauds and hypocrisies of post-war cultural Britain and
      posing against them deliberately the virtues of an aggres-
      sive nihilism."

8   ANON. "New Fiction." London <u>Times</u> (22 September), p. 15.
         Review of <u>Take A Girl Like You</u>. A sadly disappointing
      novel. The background recalls the provincial background in
      <u>Lucky Jim</u>. The characters are variants of the principle
      figures in <u>Lucky Jim</u>, but this is a dull book, twice the
      length of his first and with one quarter the gusto.

9   ANON. "The Boy Friends." <u>The Times Literary Supplement</u> (23
      September), p. 605.
         Review of <u>Take A Girl Like You</u>. Finds this novel is
      lacking in a sharp satirical eye, hilarity, and distinct
      villains. It seems Amis is changing from a "sentimental
      moralist" to a "sentimental immoralist." Concludes that the
      novel is a nasty book with nothing first-rate in it. Ex-
      cerpted in 1966.B60.

10   ANON. Review of <u>Take A Girl Like You</u>. <u>Kirkus</u>, 28 (15 December), 1042.
        Because there is little satire or humor in this novel, it is "of lesser stuff than the others in its parade of situations, its melange of peoples, its unfocused line."

11   BENTHUYSEN, ROBERT VAN. "New Books Appraised: Literature." <u>Library Journal</u>, 85 (15 February), 762.
        Brief mention of <u>New Maps of Hell</u>. "His arguments, backed by insight and a thorough knowledge of the specialty, should attract new readers and awaken young writers to the possibilities of producing quality work in this field."

12   BOWEN, JOHN. "Young Women in Bed." <u>Time & Tide</u>, 41 (24 September), 1134.
        Review of <u>Take A Girl Like You</u>. "Mr. Amis' heroes are weak, self-dramatising, self-justifying, sexually irresponsible. His heroines are stronger, wiser and nicer, but the nature of man and the nature of twentieth-century society combine to beat them in the sex war." Observes a pervading common sense. The heart of the novel is dark, but the surface is joke-filled.

13   COLEMAN, JOHN. "King of Shaft." <u>The Spectator</u>, 205 (23 September), 445-446.
        Review of <u>Take A Girl Like You</u>. Unlike the earlier novels, here a heroine faces the guilt and moral turmoil usually reserved for the male. The tirades by Graham, Martha, Edgerstoune and Patrick strike a dark, harsh note in the novel, undercutting the farce. Amis communicates exactly a disconcerting reality. However, a balance between comedy and seriousness is yet to be achieved.

14   COLVILLE, DEREK. "The Sane World of Kingsley Amis." <u>Bucknell Review</u>, 9 (March), 46-57.
        From Amis' first three novels emerges a composite hero--an honest observer of affectation and pretension. Amis' novels are pleas for sanity in a world of intellectual, artistic, literary and cultural poses. The humor is constructive. The sameness of pattern and the stock comedy endings suggest that Amis must now depart if he is to grow and develop as a writer. Concludes that in these three novels are "the seeds of Amis' growth."

15   CONNOLLY, CYRIL. "Some Pitfalls of Literary Success." London <u>Sunday Times</u> (18 September), p. 27.
        Review of <u>Take A Girl Like You</u>. An important landmark, but not as a novel. It is hard to read as a strictly comic

1960

love story, for 300 pages are devoted to "will she or won't she" be gotten by Patrick. Notes "a general tone of warm human sympathy--all taken at snailpace."

16   FACE, VERNON. "Waugh in Africa." Sphere, 243 (1 October), 34,
     Brief review of Take A Girl Like You. A funny, clever, significant book in which Amis displays "a miraculous sense of humor, an x-ray eye and that untainted appreciation of fact which made the child say that the emperor had no clothes on."

17   FORSTER, PETER. "How deep do you dig into a book?" London
     Daily Express (22 September), p. 14.
     Review of Take A Girl Like You. This novel represents an advance for Amis, away from mere entertainment toward a more serious statement.

18   FURBANK, P.N. Review of Take A Girl Like You. John O'London's
     Weekly (22 September), p. 349.
     Amis gets at the truth in the most funny and disgraceful way. "His pose of singleminded and oafish egotism lit by belated moral scruple, of righteous fury at his persecution at the hands of culture, is a splendid comic conception." Excerpted: 1966.B60.

19   GABLE, SISTER MARIELLA. "Prose Satire and the Modern Christian
     Temper." American Benediction Review, 11 (March-June), 26, 31-32.
     Amis, along with Evelyn Waugh, Aldous Huxley, Angus Wilson, Muriel Spark and Aubrey Menen, portrays society as he sees it, examining areas of human conduct where morals, values, manners and taste overlap. They all argue that society suffers from grave disorder. In Lucky Jim, however, a new type of teacher emerges. He is an "irreverent and amiable opportunist" who comes from the lower ranks of society and is envious of his academic betters. His personal tastes are often low. "Through the double vision of the phoney as seen through both Lucky Jim and Welch, the reader is made to see a new stereoscopic depth in integrity. Integrity is the value Amis consistently underlines." In That Uncertain Feeling, Amis stresses a return to moral integrity. "This moral emphasis is not satire, but its appearance in a satire on contemporary society strikes a significantly positive note."

20   GLICKSBURG, CHARLES I. "The Literature of the Angry Young Men."
     Colorado Quarterly, 8 (Spring), 295, 300-301.
     Lucky Jim is a "hilarious comedy of manners contemporary

style." In it, Amis engages in a "searching exam...of the
contemporary social scene in England," with a negative
conclusion. The structure and substance of the book is made
up of what Jim detests. "Angry," then, is a misnomer; rather, his characters are disillusioned, and it takes the form
of satire.

21   GREEN, MARTIN. <u>A Mirror for Anglo-Saxons</u>. New York: Harper
      and Row, pp. 79, 120-123, 155-157.
          Expanded reprint of 1959.B5. Amis makes us know his
      characters exactly. This ability is more important than his
      sense of comedy. Comments on Amis' gift for detail, in
      "magnifying the decent man into the figure of life and de-
      humanizing the other into simple nastiness."

22   HARTLEY, ANTHONY. "The Way We Live Now." <u>Encounter</u>, 15 (Dec-
      ember), 80-82.
          Lengthy review of <u>Take A Girl Like You</u>. The novel sur-
      prised some critics because they expected comedy and were
      not sure how to deal with a novel that has a more complex
      view of human nature and a more subtle main theme. The
      theme of the novel is how human relationships, especially
      sexual, are always imperfect and give way to unhappiness
      and often regret. The only really happy character is Julian
      Ormerod because he refuses to become involved. His role is
      to "incarnate a kindly common sense and decent feeling."
      "Patrick's cruelty, charm, and greed, combined with his ac-
      tive conscience and real humanity, make him too egocentric
      to avoid hurting Jenny the ingénue, but not sufficiently so
      to prevent himself falling in love with her or not to real-
      ise when he has hurt her." From Jenny's point of view, her
      progress is towards disillusionment. Concludes that this is
      the work of a modern novelist whose contemporary setting
      suggests contemporary ideas. "To the balance established in
      the novel between melancholy and humour corresponds an eth-
      ical balance, which leaves decency winning by a short head."

23   HATCH, ROBERT. "Lucky Jim and the Martians." <u>Nation</u>, 190
      (19 March), 257-258.
          Review of <u>New Maps of Hell</u>. An impressively substantial
      work in which Amis is more advocate than the critic. His
      study represents a "search for neat, autonomous packages of
      knowledge" which, if continued, could "produce a generation
      of complacently shallow experts."

24   HILTY, PETER. "Kingsley Amis and Mid-Century Humor." <u>Dis-
      course</u>, 3 (January), 26-45.
          Explores the stylistic devices Amis uses to achieve humor

31

1960

in his first three novels. Amis' unique and unusual meta-
phors and similes, his use of repetition and understatement,
and his parodying of cliches, all constitute the essential
elements of his style. Ironically, his failure to treat a
serious theme comes about through his successful prose style.
His first three novels have not much more than humorous intent because it is not easy to treat important ideas in
parody.

25   HOLMES, H.H. "Kingsley Amis Surveys Science Fiction." The
       New York Herald Tribune Book Review (12 June), p. 3.
          Brief review of New Maps of Hell. A clearly written,
       reliable study in which Amis honestly emphasizes science
       fiction's faults and virtues. There are a few statistical
       inaccuracies and one omission, of the influential John
       Campbell.

26   JENNINGS, ELIZABETH. "Two New Novels." Listener, 64 (6 Octo-
       ber), 591.
          Review of Take A Girl Like You. Patrick's self-analysis
       and Amis' compassion are two areas in which Amis has devel-
       oped as a novelist. His humor and compassion for people,
       especially women, is best of all. His humor is subtler and
       less negative than he had been given credit for before. Amis
       is promoting "sincerity, unselfishness, tenderness, spirit,
       and innocence," and as a moralist, he doesn't impose values
       on characters, but rather lets them find them for themselves.

27   JEPPSEN, ALLAN. "Books." Western Humanities Review, 14
       (Spring), 234-235.
          Brief review of New Maps of Hell. Amis "shows a wide
       knowledge of the genre and an unbounded confidence in its
       growth." Disagrees with Amis who says stock characters
       are part of science fiction's appeal.

28   LISTER, RICHARD. "Mr. Amis is just not the man for middle-aged
       squares." London Evening Standard (27 September), p. 17.
          Review of Take A Girl Like You. Amis has developed a
       more complex novel. The point of view is not limited to
       only one central character, and the ramifications of the
       sexual pursuit are more involved.

29   McCARY, ROBERT. Review of New Maps of Hell. San Francisco
       Chronicle (20 March), p. 16.
          Amis is composed almost entirely of prejudices, but be-
       neath them he makes some sharp points.

30   MILLER, KARL. "Girl, with Tigers." The Observer (18 September), p. 26.
        Review of Take A Girl Like You. The theme is sex.
Jenny Bunn is the "sweet and guileless" heroine. Humor is
more closely tied to the fundamental story this time. As
usual, many jokes are aimed at Amis' aversions. Although
the jokes are assigned to Patrick, ultimately the joke is
on Patrick himself. The mystery behind Patrick's dealings
with Jenny derives from the conflict between Patrick's li-
centiousness and the feelings of severity, seen in his jokes
and brutal exploits. We are left with the idea that any
permanent mating will have "something permanently bitter and
irresolute about it." Concludes that the role of Jenny's
innocence is worked a little too hard.

31   NEWMAN, JAMES R. "Books: An examination of the history and
        the present state of science fiction." Scientific American,
        203 (July), 179-184.
        Review of New Maps of Hell. This is a "thoughtful, wholly
unpretentious, amusing and self-amused survey of a branch
of writing that deserves just such treatment." Summarizes
Amis' major points.

32   NOON, WILLIAM T., S.J. "Satire: Poison and the Professor."
        English Record, 11 (Fall), 53-56.
        Records a meeting with Amis, in which Amis says he doubts
Lucky Jim is a satire of the British Academic scene.

33   OREL, HAROLD. "Amis in the Underworld." Yale Review, 40
        (June), 602-604.
        Review of New Maps of Hell. Notes that Amis doesn't
exaggerate the virtues of science fiction. He presents an
optimistic, reasonable view. This is an important book because science fiction is such a popular field. Amis' interest in popular art forms is ignored by scholars and critics.

34   PELLING, HENRY. "Reconstruction, 1945-55," in Modern Britain:
        1885-1955. Edinburgh: Thomas Nelson and Sons, p. 187.
        As a new novelist Amis, like John Wain, commented spe-
cifically on the new post-war world.

35   PESCHMANN, HERMAN. "The Nonconformists, Angry Young Men,
        Lucky Jims, and Outsiders." English (London), 13 (Winter),
        12-16.
        Notes that Lucky Jim is more than a superb piece of satire.
It is also the study of a grammar-school boy who has made
good. Observes the ironic distance of Amis in Socialism

1960

<u>and the Intellectuals</u>. Amis is not very angry; the "Angry
Young Man" label is inaccurate.

36   PRICE, R.G.G. "New Novels." <u>Punch</u>, 239 (28 September), 467–
      468.
          Review of <u>Take A Girl Like You</u>. This is Amis' best novel
      so far. In its convivialities, urban landscapes, caricature
      at times, and high spirits, the novel parallels Dickens, but
      the problem of conduct is more complicated for Amis.

37   ROPER, DEREK. "Tradition and Innovation in the Occidental
      Lyric of the Last Decade. 1, English Poetry and the Tradition,
      1950–60." <u>Books Abroad</u>, 34 (Autumn), 344–347.
          Amis' poetry is distinguished by light verse, amusing
      conversation, irreverence. Rarely is there any depth or
      complexity in the experience discussed in the poems or in
      his response to it.

38   SHRAPNEL, NORMAN. "Soft at the Centre?" <u>Manchester Guardian</u>
      (23 September), p. 8.
          Review of <u>Take A Girl Like You</u>. Patrick is the New Hero
      a bit older. He has changed, but not for the better. He
      has lost his class consciousness, which is a good point,
      but he is more baffling. The comedy stems from the old
      story of a man not being up to his own standards. Does see
      signs of warmth and sympathy that may emerge in later novels.
      Reprinted: 1960.B39.

39   _____. "Soft at the Centre?" <u>Manchester Guardian Weekly</u>, 83
      (29 September), p. 12.
          Reprint of 1960.B38.

40   SOUVAGE, JACQUES. "The Unresolved Tension: An Interpretation
      of Iris Murdoch's <u>Under the Net</u>." <u>Révue Des Langues Vivantes</u>,
      26 (May), 425.
          Mentions <u>Lucky Jim</u> as a non-humanistic novel.

41   WILLIAMS, CHRISTOPHER. "The State of English Poetry." <u>The</u>
      <u>Twentieth Century</u>, 168 (November), 438–439.
          As a poet, Amis has nothing to write about, so he makes
      it up with irony and craftsmanship. The language is arti-
      ficial and his "main instrument of evasion." Amis is a
      self-conscious writer, "<u>afraid</u> of the rôle of intellectual
      or poet."

42   WOOD, FREDERICK T. "Current Literature 1958." <u>English Studies</u>,
      41 (February), 49–50.
          Review of <u>I Like It Here</u>. A disappointing picaresque

novel with some good characterization. Praises Amis for
his patience with "erring humanity." Criticizes his mockery
of culture and refinement all the time, which seems forced.

43   YAFFEE, JAMES. "The Modern Trend Toward Meaningful Martians."
      Saturday Review, 43 (April), 22.
          Review of New Maps of Hell. An entertaining book whose
      thesis "is all too indicative of the dismal tendency of our
      times." Says it is a mistake to judge science fiction by
      the standards of literature.

1961 A BOOKS - NONE

1961 B SHORTER WRITINGS

1   ANON. "Literature of the Future." London Times (16 February),
         p. 15.
          Review of New Maps of Hell. Amis separates science fic-
      tion from fantasy, indicates its satire, and points to its
      themes on the hopes and fears of mankind. Science fiction
      may be the literature of the future in more than one sense.

2   ANON. "Science Fiction." The Times Literary Supplement (17
         February), p. 108.
          Review of New Maps of Hell. An infectious book and a
      fair study. Some stories, Amis points out, are literate,
      inventive, and sententious.

3   ANON. "Slap and a Tickle." Newsweek, 57 (27 February), 93-94.
          Review of Take A Girl Like You. If it were not for Amis'
      "pervasive comic insight and sense of proportion," this
      would be just another novel on sex.

4   ANON. "Mixed Fiction." Time, 77 (10 March), 102.
          Review of Take A Girl Like You. A serio-comic novel
      that is rather disappointing. Amis "remains a shrewd, ac-
      curate observer of what sociologists call courtship patterns."

5   ANON. "Fiction." Booklist, 57 (15 March), 448.
          Review of Take A Girl Like You. "A witty, precise, some-
      times racy novel overflowing with exuberant characters and
      conversation."

6   ANON. "Notional Worlds." The Times Literary Supplement (13
         October), p. 679.
          Brief review of Spectrum I. A collection of "intellectual
      fantasies." The introduction is particularly good.

35

1961

7   ANON. "Notes on Current Books." <u>Virginia Quarterly Review</u>,
         37 (Autumn), cxviii.
              Review of <u>Take A Girl Like You</u>. "An honest and serious
         study of the difficult relationship between a man who
         doesn't want marriage and a girl who won't give in without
         marriage." This is <u>Pamela</u> updated by Amis' "wry humour and
         keen eye for current mores."

8   BERGONZI, BERNARD. "Science Fiction in Orbit." <u>Manchester</u>
         <u>Guardian</u> (17 February), p. 7.
              Review of <u>New Maps of Hell</u>. An informative, entertaining
         study marred by a "joky defensiveness" and an approach
         aimed primarily at American readers. Amis mistakenly sees
         William Golding as a science fiction writer, and he blurs
         the distinction between fantasy and science fiction proper.
         Reprinted: 1961.B9.

9   _____. "Science Fiction in Orbit." <u>Manchester Guardian</u>
         <u>Weekly</u>, 84 (23 February), 11.
              Reprint of 1961.B18.

10   BIRSTEIN, ANN. "Round Peg, Square World." <u>Reporter</u>, 24 (13
         April), 55-56.
              Review of <u>Take A Girl Like You</u>. Patrick Standish calls
         to mind earlier heroes. Like them, he is despised by offi-
         cialdom, led astray by friends, and sees sex become a fan-
         tasy nightmare. His point of view becomes pretty depressing.
         He is, as a comic type, a schlemiel and among Amis' most
         vivid characters. There is some question whether or not
         Patrick deserves the trouble he gets into.

11   BLIVEN, NAOMI. "Fallen Angel." <u>New Yorker</u>, 37 (15 April),
         162.
              Review of <u>Take A Girl Like You</u>. More lifelike than
         <u>Lucky Jim</u>. Amis shows great understanding of Jenny's point
         of view, and "records a segment of the contemporary scene
         with brisk, entertaining fidelity." This is the classic
         theme of love in conflict with love.

12   BRIEN, ALAN. "Monster Babies." <u>The Spectator</u>, 207 (27 Octo-
         ber), 600.
              Brief mention of <u>Spectrum I</u>. A collection of "some of
         the best and worst in the genre."

13   BRYDEN, RONALD. "British Fiction 1959-1960," in <u>International</u>
         <u>Literary Annual No. 3</u>. Edited by Arthur Boyars and Pamela
         Lyon. London: John Calder, p. 44.
              Contemporary British novels are concerned with a

reexamination and redefinition of British society from the ground up. Both Amis and John Wain share affinities with the work of an older generation, who found a middle way between "hazards of conformity and rebellion in the various bohemias between the wars."

14   COLEMAN, JOHN. "Infernos and Utopias." London <u>Sun Times</u> (12 February), p. 26.
       Review of <u>New Maps of Hell</u>. An "entertaining and intelligent survey of science fiction." Complains that there is not enough good science fiction to justify a study of this length.

15   COSMAN, MAX. "Take A Novelist Like Amis." <u>Commonweal</u>, 73 (10 March), 615.
       Review of <u>Take A Girl Like You</u>. It is difficult to tell when Amis is or is not being satirical. Theme seems to be the need to accept what matures us. The conclusion is unconvincing. Amis seems uncertain about his approach.

16   CURLE, J.J. "Utopia Limited." <u>Tablet</u>, 215 (4 March), 205.
       Review of <u>New Maps of Hell</u>. Ambiguous in the appeal of the subject and in the author's response. Amis enjoys the story, but as a technician he can't help pointing out the flaws.

17   ENRIGHT, D.J. "The New Pastoral-Comical." <u>The Spectator</u>, 206 (3 February), 154-155.
       Review of <u>Take A Girl Like You</u>. Contrasts the novel to William Cooper's <u>Scenes from Married Life</u>. Dislikes the malice and savagery with which Amis treats his characters and their environment. "Mr. Amis would be a master of the sneer if the sneer weren't master of him."

18   GLICK, NATHAN. "Writing up the Social Ladder." <u>New Leader</u>, 44 (27 November), 29-30.
       Review of <u>Take A Girl Like You</u>. Like earlier heroes, Patrick thumbs his nose at the tastes, values and language of the Establishment. Jenny is a "likable young woman, without pretense." Amis is a "repressed but incorrigible romantic, and the tension between programmatic amoralism and lurking idealism gives his books their internal drama and their saving humanity."

19   GOLDING, WILLIAM. "Androids All." <u>The Spectator</u>, 206 (24 February), 263-264.
       Review of <u>New Maps of Hell</u> in which he calls the study "more analytical than evaluative."

1961

20 GREEN, MARTIN. "British Comedy and the British Sense of Humor: Shaw, Waugh and Amis." Texas Quarterly, 7 (Fall), 217-227.
    Notes that Amis' humor is much more thoroughly moral than Shaw's or Waugh's. It is "essentially concerned with self-questioning and self-criticism, with the difficulties of the sexual life, and with emotional and intellectual sincerity." Amis has, in fact, begun to create a sense of humor for the "Lawrentian, relatively inarticulate, half of Britain." However, his sense of humor is still rudimentary, and he has not produced anything close to the brilliance of Shaw and Waugh.

21 HARTLEY, L.P. "Book Reviews." London Magazine, OS 8 (January), 72.
    Review of Take A Girl Like You. Amis' real interest in this novel is the social satire of people whose main interests are sex, drink and cars. Amis doesn't really care what happens to Jenny Bunn.

22 HEPPENSTALL, RAYNER. The Fourfold Tradition: Notes on the French and English Literatures. London: Barrie and Rockliff, pp. 213-225, 244-246.
    It is hard to dissociate Amis from his heroes. Amis' comedy is similar to and yet different from the comedy of Evelyn Waugh. Discusses Amis' "anti-style."

23 HYNES, SAMUEL. "What To Do When Everything's Permitted?" The New York Times Book Review (26 February), p. 4.
    Review of Take A Girl Like You with some general comments about the development of Amis' characters in all four novels. Amis finds little matter for comic invention in his study of sexual morality. His latest novel is uncomical; hopefully, he will return to being funny now.

24 JENNINGS, ELIZABETH. "Poetry To-Day," in Poetry Today. London: Longmans, Green for the British Council, pp. 9-11.
    Offers observations about the Movement poets and Amis' contributions to the group. Amis shares with Philip Larkin and D.J. Enright "a wry, careful, mildly debunking tone." They were anxious "not to appear gullible, emotional or sentimental." They eschewed abstraction, confusion and obscurity and sought clarity, respect for the language, a "calm voice" and feelings ruled by the intellect. "They devised no world-schemes, no personal philosophies, and would have nothing to do with the symbolic or the allegorical."

25 KING, FRANCIS. "Smog of the Spirit." <u>New Statesman</u>, 62 (13 October), 525.
     Brief mention of <u>Spectrum I</u>.

26 LEACH, GERALD. "Scientific opium." <u>Time & Tide</u>, 42 (25 February), 284.
     Review of <u>New Maps of Hell</u>. This book may well be "the turning point in science fiction's bid for respectability and general acceptance as serious literature." Amis defines the medium, traces the history, and surveys current attitudes and themes.

27 LIGHT, JAMES F. "Reviews: A Motley Sextet." <u>Minnesota Review</u>, 2 (Fall), 108-110.
     Review of <u>Take A Girl Like You</u>. Notes that seriousness dominates the comedy in this novel. Although Amis mocks unattractive people, he shows a greater awareness of their pathos. Notes a greater humaneness in Amis as he satirizes an English society caught between two moral worlds: "a strife between the egoism and hedonism of the new mucker bastard and the conventions of the established way."

28 MALOFF, SAUL. "The Contemporary British Comic Novel." <u>Saturday Review</u>, 44 (8 April), 26.
     Review of <u>Take A Girl Like You</u>. Concludes that Amis is at his strongest when writing comedy of manners. He is an uncanny observer who, by describing, locates with precision. This defining observation keeps the reader interested above and beyond the plot.

29 MELIK, PETER. "Modern Vocations." <u>National Review</u>, 10 (8 April), 221-222.
     Review of <u>Take A Girl Like You</u>. Patrick Standish's chase of Jenny Bunn is "sharp-witted, occasionally tender, and frequently ruthless." The ending is a little too true to be good. Virginity and marriage are outmoded relationships now; for Patrick, they died around 1914. For Jenny, it's "somewhere between a class sentiment and a racial memory. But for neither is it an organic, outside reality which can ordain right behavior."

30 MOERS, ELLEN. "Still Angry." <u>Commentary</u>, 31 (June), 542-544.
     Review of <u>Take A Girl Like You</u>. Notes a similarity in theme to William Cooper's <u>Scenes from Provincial Life</u>, but not in quality. Jenny is the most serious, most successful character here, and except for her, the book is imperfect and unfinished. There is no self-pity with Amis. His pivotal characters are doomed to a troubled maturity. Observes

1961

that Amis escapes "mere snob concerns." His highest comedy
stems from excursions into the "imaginary life of ineffec-
tual people....They touch on the human condition which
traps us all--upper, middle, or petty in class." Despite
their rebelliousness, his heroes have no complaint against
the sub-structure of their society.

31 MOON, ERIC. "New Books Appraised: Fiction." Library Journal,
    86 (1 January), 109.
        Brief review of Take A Girl Like You. There is less wit
    in this novel. It is a sad novel in which Amis strains for
    humor. A boring book riddled with clichés and caricatures.

32 MUDRICK, MARVIN. "Something to Say." Hudson Review, 14 (Sum-
    mer), 291-292.
        Review of Take A Girl Like You. This is an update of
    Clarissa with a weak plot and a lack of comedy or suspense.
    Patrick Standish's suffering from fear of age, decay and
    death is the only interesting aspect.

33 OLIPHANT, ROBERT. "Public Voices and Wise Guys." Virginia
    Quarterly Review, 37 (Autumn), 525-526.
        "One measure of the vitality of the contemporary novel
    might well be the extent to which the conventions of lan-
    guage are adapted and reshaped." Like Salinger's Catcher
    in The Rye, Amis in Lucky Jim makes clear that "the appar-
    ently indirect relationship between author, statement, and
    central character turns out to be a direct relationship.
    Though the texture of such a novel is richer, the author is
    nevertheless using an essentially simple public voice."

34 PARKER, R.B. "Farce and Society: the Range of Kingsley Amis."
    Wisconsin Studies in Contemporary Literature, 2 (Fall)
    27-38.
        Review of Take A Girl Like You. This novel represents
    a new departure for Amis, for he leaves behind the pattern
    of the first three novels to focus on a heroine. It is a
    denser novel in terms of realistic description and moral and
    social significance of events. Amis seems to be trying a
    new mixture of farce and social comment, with emphasis on
    the latter. But because Amis implies through technique that
    the realities of present-day England are illusory, clichés,
    much of the political and social comment is undercut and
    the novel ends up ambiguous.

35 POORE, CHARLES. "Books of the Times." The New York Times
    (23 February), p. 25.
        Review of Take A Girl Like You. This is a morality play

in novel form on manners and morals in contemporary England.
The main plot would have made a good short story. Through
inventive characterization and satirical comment on personal
and public affairs, Amis develops one of his funniest novels.

36   PRITCHETT, V.S. "The Know-alls." New Statesman, 61 (17 Feb-
        ruary), 226.
            Review of New Maps of Hell. Objects to the "know-all
        side of science fiction" in this study. The most interesting
        chapter concerns the utopias.

37   RILEY, PHILLIP. "Cinema: That Uncertain Feeling." London
        Magazine, OS 8 (August), 74-78.
            Reports on the filming of That Uncertain Feeling. Finds
        it difficult to adapt the novel to the screen because the
        plot is weak and much of the humor comes from descriptive
        passages. Thus, the writer of the script changed emphasis
        from situation comedy or description to comic dialogue.
        Notes that more is made of Lewis' family life; two major
        farcical scenes are changed; the competition for the job is
        increased, and the serious note at the end is leavened.

38   ROLO, CHARLES. "Reader's Choice: Varieties of Experience."
        Atlantic Monthly, 207 (April), 114.
            Review of Take A Girl Like You. This is Amis' best book
        so far. Notes a more serious and complex view of life mixed
        with a flair for farce. Through the characters, Amis main-
        tains a balance between sadness and humor. Novel advocates
        decent behavior, especially in the sexual relationships.

39   ROSS, T.J. "Lucky Jenny, or Affluent Times." New Republic,
        144 (27 March), 21-23.
            Review of Take A Girl Like You. This is Amis' most
        "glamorous novel so far. It's a true romance." Discusses
        Amis' use of doubles in characterization, and says the nov-
        el is a study of Jenny Bunn's culture.

40   SCOTT-KILVERT, IAN. "English Fiction 1958-1960, II." British
        Book News, no. 248 (April), p. 238.
            Amis' novels are comedies of attitudes, emphasizing po-
        sitions rather than telling a plausible story. His style
        is "slangy" with a "belligerent tone."

41   SNOW, C.P. "Italia Suevo: Forerunner of Cooper and Amis."
        Essays and Studies, 14 (Spring), 7-16.
            Notes that the Italian novelist Suevo's quality of truth-
        fulness and absolute candor was transmitted to an entire

1961

stream of novels, including William Cooper's and the best
of Amis' work.

42   SPECTOR, ROBERT DONALD. "Amis's Comic Satire of A Good Girl
     in a Wolfish World." New York Herald Tribune Lively Arts
     and Book Review (26 February), p. 28.
         Brief review of Take A Girl Like You. A satire on the
     innocent country girl visiting the big city for the first
     time. Relates this to Amis' earlier satires.

43   THOMPSON, JOHN. "Plot, Character, Etc." Partisan Review,
     no. 5/6 (Spring), pp. 707-710.
         Review of Take A Girl Like You. Like Iris Murdoch's A
     Severed Head, Amis' novel is productive and successful be-
     cause both are comic novels, use the traditional machinery
     of fiction, and yet are very up-to-date.

44   WARNKE, F.J. "Some Recent Novels: A Variety of Worlds."
     Yale Review, 50 (June), 630-631.
         Review of Take A Girl Like You. Represents a larger
     range for Amis, for the problems confronted are more serious
     and he is now working with two central characters. However,
     the moral implications about whether Jenny Bunn will sleep
     with Patrick Standish are not as important as Amis would
     have us believe. His attitude towards this incident is
     uncertain.

45   WEATHERBY, W.J. "Mr. Sellers and Mr. Amis: A Conversation
     Reported by W.J. Weatherby." Manchester Guardian (27 April),
     p. 9.
         Discussion between Amis and Peter Sellers on comedy and
     film during the filming of Take A Girl Like You. Amis says
     it's hard adapting the novel to the screen. He sees more
     social comment coming in films. "'I think one of the im-
     portant things we are approaching is real serio-comedy. We
     are getting to the point of mixing humour and seriousness
     much more thoroughly.'" Sellers responds by saying that
     this mixture is "'essential because that's really what hap-
     pens in life.'" Goes on to say that much of what people do
     looks ludicrous, so the writer must play it down to make it
     seem credible. Thus, it is very easy to "'institutionalise
     life.'" Amis says he would like to see "'a mixture of fan-
     tasy, clowning, and social comment.'"

46   WILSON, ANGUS. "The Status of Science Fiction." The Observer
     (21 March), p. 28.
         Brief review of New Maps of Hell with a summary of the
     contents.

47   WOOD, FREDERICK T. "Current Literature, 1960." English
        Studies, 42 (August), 260.
           Review of Take A Girl Like You. Suffers from a diffuse
     plot and superficial characters. It is an unconvincing
     novel, ambiguous in intent, and "far removed from the natu-
     ralness and spontaneity" of Amis' earlier works.

48   YOUNG, B.A. "Science-Fiction As One Of The Fine Arts." Punch,
        240 (2 February), 333.
           Review of New Maps of Hell. Unfortunately, Amis excludes
     fantasy and "space-opera." The most important chapter is
     that in which he examines how science fiction writers deal
     with sex, politics, religion, art, and what kinds of worlds
     take form in their writings.

49   _____. "Space-Time." Punch, 241 (8 November), 697.
        Brief mention of Spectrum I.

1962 A BOOKS - NONE

1962 B SHORTER WRITINGS

1   ANON. "Short Stories." London Times (20 September), p. 15
           Review of Spectrum I. The main moral of the stories is
     it's best to be tough as well as decent. Also, "we should
     leave people alone to do what they like, that if our feelings
     dry up we become ridiculous and imperceptive, and that it
     pays to try to fit in wherever we may be." The last story
     is the best, for it "reveals a wider range of effect and a
     new subtlety to add to his grip of narrative, dialogue, and
     plot." In the other stories, the characters are sketches,
     often caricatures, and "his moral universe a narrow, grey
     place, where vulgarity must be good and the best we can hope
     for is the occasional night out."

2   ANON. "Human Interest." The Times Literary Supplement (21
        September), p. 706.
           Review of Spectrum I. Most of the stories have a moral.
     These are humane stories, and reflect our post-war world in
     sound of speech, cant, goodness, values, and disenchantment.

3   ANON. "Facing The Future." The Times Literary Supplement (5
        October), p. 781.
           Brief mention of Spectrum II. Likes the last seven
     stories.

1962

4   ANON. "Mr. Amis Resigns Fellowship." London <u>Times</u> (21 December), p. 11.
    Account explaining why Amis left Cambridge. Says he doesn't like the formality of faculty life and the excessive amount of protocol.

5   BALL, PATRICIA. "The Photographic Art." <u>A Review of English Literature</u>, 3 (June), 50-52.
    Notes the honesty of Amis' work in <u>A Case of Samples</u>, and points out the realities drawn attention to in two poems.

6   BENTLEY, W.E. "Science Fiction." <u>Essays In Criticism</u>, 12 (April), 203-207.
    Review of <u>New Maps of Hell</u>. Amis argues that there is a frontier between the two worlds of fiction, science fiction and literature. To say that science fiction is about things can't be an excuse for its excesses or a criticism of them, however.

7   CHARLES, GERDA. "B. Malamud--the 'Natural' Writer." <u>Jewish Quarterly</u> (Spring), pp. 5-6.
    Brief mention of the comparable qualities of a Malamud character to Jim Dixon.

8   CONQUEST, ROBERT. "Dragons and All Deeps." <u>Encounter</u>, 18 (May), 77-80.
    Review of <u>New Maps of Hell</u>. Amis' assertion here is revolutionary, for he argues that our tradition of fiction is inadequate. Discusses Amis' assertion that science fiction fills a need not catered to by the mainstream of literature.

9   DAVENPORT, JOHN. "Dark Glasses." <u>The Spectator</u>, 209 (19 October), 603-604.
    Review of <u>My Enemy's Enemy</u>. The stories reveal a nightmarish world in "more sad than savage" stories, making us feel the human condition is hopeless. "One feels that Mr. Amis would like people to be different, less socially awkward, less spiritually threadbare, more loving; but he permits himself no Chekhovian licence."

10 DERRICK, CHRISTOPHER. "Not Proven." <u>Tablet</u>, 216 (20 October), 988.
    Review of <u>My Enemy's Enemy</u>. Some aspects of this collection make it into Tory propaganda. The war stories evoke the political mood of 1945. In "Interesting Things," Amis' comedy shows through. "It all seems rather a waste; none the less, there is something very pleasantly restful about

1962

a short visit to a country where the cheerful questions of
guilt and innocence never arise at all."

11   FRIERDENBERG, EDGAR Z.   "The Establishment of Self-Esteem," in
      his The Vanishing Adolescent.   New York: Dell, p. 82.
          Sees Jim Dixon as a hero who is unsure of himself and
      hence vulnerable.

12   GINDIN, JAMES.   "Kingsley Amis' Funny Novels," in his Postwar
      British Fiction: New Accents and Attitudes.   Berkeley and
      Los Angeles: University of California Press, pp. 34-50.
          In his first four novels, Amis erects a whole comic
      world based upon word play, verbal jokes, incongruous comic
      images, digressions, irrelevancies, and role-playing.   The
      point of view is a comic acceptance "of the contemporary
      world as it is."   The verbal texture that is essentially
      comic provides the unity in his fiction.   The moral issues
      don't follow clear or consistent lines, however.   Amis'
      theme is adjustment to society.   Notes a gradual disappear-
      ance of the bumbling, self-conscious hero.   Excerpted:
      1974.B33.

13   GROSS, JOHN.   "Makes You Sober."   New Statesman, 64 (21 Sep-
      tember), 363-364.
          Review of My Enemy's Enemy.   Amis grows more realistic
      and more moral as he progresses, but his comedy becomes
      more unreal and morally objectionable.   Characters become
      nastier.   Notes an "unlocated sense of horror" more and
      more frequently.   Says that realism and moralism have all
      along undermined the comedy.

14   HOLLOWAY, JOHN.   "Tank in the Stalls: Notes on the 'School of
      Anger,'" in his The Charted Mirror.   New York: Horizon Press,
      pp. 137-145.
          Reprint of 1957.B10. Also reprinted in 1959.B4.

15   HOOK, ANDREW, ed.   "day five: the novel and the future," in
      The Novel Today.   Edinburgh: International Writers' Con-
      ference, p. 61.
          Brief interview in which Amis comments on the future of
      the novel.   Expects to see "some sort of blending of the
      serious novel with more popular forms," such as science
      fiction.

16   HUTCHENS, JOHN K.   "Science Fiction: Two Books."   The New
      York Herald Tribune (11 April), p. 29
          Review of Spectrum I.   "With only a couple of exceptions

45

1962

[these stories] are windy and overwritten, and the gadgets clank tinnily."

17 JENKINS, PRISCILLA. "the contemporary english novel," in The Novel Today. Edited by Andrew Hook. Edinburgh: International Writers' Conference, p. 87.
    In spite of the great differences in temperament between them, Amis and his contemporaries demonstrate a trend in English fiction at the moment, and that is to "show a sociological understanding of contemporary English life and treat it with strict realism." Notes a superficiality in Amis; he is realistic only in the narrowest sense. This is noticeable in Lucky Jim and Take A Girl Like You, where Amis never explores Jenny Bunn's desire to keep her virginity; thus, "one is uncertain whether he intends the loss of it to seem pointless or...an acceptance of the compromises of grown-up life." Like the others, Amis fails to investigate "questions of value and motive."

18 KARL, FREDERICK R. "The Angries: Is There a Protestant in the House?" in his A Reader's Guide to the Contemporary English Novel. New York: Farrar, Straus and Giroux, pp. 221-228, 231.
    Jim Dixon is representative of the younger heroes of the 1950's; however, he's angry about "straw dummies," and his revolt is meaningless. The incidents and characters are superficial, and Dixon is more of a music hall character than a rebel. That Uncertain Feeling and I Like It Here are sketchy novels. Take A Girl Like You merely repeats, through Jenny Bunn, what Dixon and Lewis have already said.

19 LERNER, LAURENCE. "New Fiction." The Listener, 68 (20 September), 449.
    Review of My Enemy's Enemy. Except for the science fiction story at the end, all of the stories are topical realism. They differ from Amis' novels in that they are not funny. Many, in fact, seem to be leftovers. The army stories do show a seriousness and honesty that is admirable. In "Moral Fibre," Amis is observant, but he goes nowhere with the story; the moral is muddled. Concludes that perhaps Amis is best when funny.

20 LEVINE, NORMAN. "Amis in Arms." London Sunday Times (23 September), p. 29.
    Review of My Enemy's Enemy. In the army stories, Amis' obsession with class comes across strongly. Although the stories hinge on insights into human behavior, the characters are often "class puppets." "Interesting Things" is

46

the most successful story, for with it the reader will
recall similar experiences he has had. Although Amis deals
in trivialities in these stories, his strength is that he
writes in a simple style, so that when "out-of-the-ordinary
perceptions" do appear, they assume extraordinary depth.

21 LODGE, DAVID. "The Contemporary Novel and All that Jazz."
    The London Magazine, NS 2 (August), 75-76.
        Although peripheral to the main theme of Take A Girl
    Like You, jazz does function as a character-building ele-
    ment. Notes Patrick Standish's nostalgia for the simple
    forms of jazz, and says his discriminations are an index of
    his intelligence and sophistication.

22 O'CONNOR, WILLIAM VAN. "Two Types of 'Heroes' in Post War
    British Fiction." Publication of the Modern Language Asso-
    ciation, 77 (March), 168-174.
        Since World War II, a new protagonist has appeared in the
    British novel, one who is seedy, ineffectual, and comic;
    one who is involved in a "half-hearted contest with society,
    especially with the Establishment." Unlike the nineteenth
    century sensitive esthete who pursued the arts in lonely
    isolation, this hero experiences a new form of alienation.

23 PENN, RICHARD. "Latest Novels." Time & Tide, 43 (4 October),
    25.
        Review of My Enemy's Enemy. Amis' comedy is at its peak;
    his exposure of "affectation and unpleasant personal habits
    is merciless."

24 PRESS, JOHN. "English Verse Since 1945," in Essays by Divers
    Hands. Vol. 31. Edited by Peter Green. London and New York:
    Oxford University Press, pp. 163-165.
        In his poetry, Amis seeks to obliterate all that is
    "loose, careless, sloppily made." Comments on Amis' "con-
    tempt for all forms of humbug, his cool, astringent obser-
    vation of human nature, and his technical adroitness."

25 PRICE, R.G.G. "New Fiction." Punch, 243 (3 October), 504.
        Review of My Enemy's Enemy. Notes a maturing compassion
    in the army stories. "For the first time he seems equally
    aware of the forces operating on all his characters." "All
    the Blood Within Me" is brilliant.

26 QUINTANA, RICHARD. "Book Reviews." Wisconsin Studies in Con-
    temporary Literature, 3 (Winter), 81-83.
        Amis has suffered a loss of direction since Lucky Jim.
    Take A Girl Like You leaves the reader feeling uncomfortable

1962

because of the attempt to mix comedy and seriousness and
because of an uncertainty about Amis' intentions. It's unclear whether Amis intends Patrick to be a modern Tom Jones,
or whether the novel is a satire on Pamela.

27   QUINTON, ANTHONY. "Forget and Forgive." London Sunday Telegraph (23 September), p. 9.
Brief review of My Enemy's Enemy, including a summary
of its contents.

28   ROSS, ALAN. "Special Notices." London Magazine, NS 2 (December), 85.
Review of My Enemy's Enemy. Amis' narrative gift and
"his unique eye for microscopic detail" are evidenced in
this collection. The army stories are the best, for there
he never lapses into self-indulgent farce.

29   SAGAR, KEITH. "Science Fiction." London Sunday Times (16
September), p. 26.
Brief mention of Spectrum II.

30   SILVERLIGHT, JOHN. "Kingsley Amis: The Writer, the Symbol."
The New York Herald Tribune Book Review (21 January), p. 6.
Reprint of 1962.B31.

31   _____. "Profile: Kingsley Amis." The Observer (14 January),
p. 13.
Amis comments in an interview on his parents, education,
and method of writing. Reprinted: 1962.B30.

32   SPENDER, STEPHEN. "Moderns and Contemporaries." The Listener,
68 (11 October), 555-556.
Seeks to differentiate between the generations of James
Joyce and Amis. Replied to in 1965.B35.

33   STURGEON, THEODORE. "Literati vs. Cognoscenti." National
Review, 13 (23 October), 321-322.
Review of Spectrum I. Notes a low quality from some of
the best writers in this collection. The net impression is
that the editors, "in their dedicated disinterest in style,
form, and cadence, are tone-deaf."

34   TOYNBEE, PHILIP. "From Virgil to Kingsley Amis." The Observer
(22 April), p. 20.
Review of Penguin Modern Poets. Amis is little more than
a "fairly skilled technician" in this collection.

35   WAIN, JOHN. <u>Sprightly Running: Part of an Autobiography</u>.
      New York and London: Macmillan, pp. 169, 188, 203-205.
           Recounts his friendship with Amis during their days at
      Oxford and the influence Amis, as a writer, had on him.
      Says Amis' vision of life "is based on a steadying common
      sense, a real hatred of imbalance and excess."

36   WYNDHAM, FRANCIS. "Towards A Stiff Upper Lip." <u>The Observer</u>
      (23 September), p. 25.
           Review of <u>My Enemy's Enemy</u>. The military stories drama-
      tize the "pettiness engendered by military life." The
      characters are obsessed "by tiny problems affecting their
      status, by suspected affronts to their dignity and by fear
      of giving social offence." In "Moral Fibre," Amis shows
      John Lewis preaching against interfering do-gooders. The
      exaggeration and unfairness in Amis' depiction of a social
      worker's insensitivity is typical of Amis. Praises Amis'
      ear for exact speech and his skilled pacing of the narrative.
      Only occasionally is Amis guilty of an "overly conscious
      hostility to literary pretentiousness which becomes
      facetious."

37   YOUNG, B.A. "Space-Time." <u>Punch</u>, 243 (19 September), 433.
      Brief mention of <u>Spectrum</u> II.

1963 A BOOKS - NONE

1963 B SHORTER WRITINGS

1   ANON. "Pathway To Parnassus." <u>The Times Literary Supplement</u>
      (26 July), p. 557.
           Review of <u>The Evans Country</u>. Amis is a sour comic who
      catches "the intonation of demotic English and its Welsh
      variants" in Evans. "A robust and randy comedian, with a
      richly entertaining technical skill, he has the ability to
      make one enjoy and even like the very characters he exposes
      by his guying ridicule."

2   ANON. "Fantasia." <u>The Times Literary Supplement</u> (25 October).
      p. 866.
           Brief mention of <u>Spectrum III</u>. The collection shows the
      editors' preference for tales of action and technique.

3   ANON. "Iago and America." <u>The Times Literary Supplement</u> (14
      November), p. 921.
           Review of <u>One Fat Englishman</u>. This is the best satire
      of wit and intelligence. Everything is portrayed through

1963

Micheldene's eyes, who at a glance can pick out the ridiculous features of anything he looks at. Slowly the reader
realizes how gross and stupid his snobbery is. "As the
general decency and good will of the majority of the Americans he meets becomes plainer--as his own discomfiture by
them, rather than their discomfiture by him, proves more
and more to be the outcome of his bland and beastly sallies,"
the reader loses sympathy with him. The novel recalls
Amis' epigraph to Take A Girl Like You; here, Roger is the
ape in hell. He is a tragi-comic Iago, for "the only things
he enjoys doing are those that end in harm, discord and tor-
ment." Also notes that Roger's physical agonies have an
analogy to pains within the soul, so this "marks the first
clear effort Mr. Amis has yet made at locating the roots of
human misery."

4   ANON. "New Fiction." London Times (14 November), p. 17.
        Review of One Fat Englishman. Finds Micheldene "lumpy
    with prejudices and unblinkingly self-assertive." As the
    anti-hero, he "seems designed to illustrate the theory that
    the innocents at home are by no means as innocent as they
    seem abroad." Although we see affluent society, the people
    are poor "in that they have an average emotional age of
    about two and a half."

5   BEMIS, R. "Books in Brief." National Review, 15 (July), 73.
        Brief mention of My Enemy's Enemy, which he calls an
    "uncommonly serious" work.

6   BRADBURY, MALCOLM. "The Nasty Hero." Punch, 245 (20 April),
    245.
        Review of One Fat Englishman. Micheldene is Jim Dixon
    turned sour. Finds hints of comic tragedy as the plot de-
    velops by way of sexual pursuits and a religious theme.
    This is an incomplete novel, for the moral apparatus doesn't
    relate to the latter action.

7   COLEMAN, JOHN. "In pursuit of the unspeakable." Manchester
    Guardian (15 November), p. 8.
        Review of One Fat Englishman. Roger is typical of ear-
    lier Amis villains. The other targets, Americans, come out
    more wholesome and concerned than they would if he were not
    there. Macher is the most cruelly selfish.

8   CONQUEST, ROBERT. "Lyrical Larynxes." The Spectator, 211
    (26 July), 114.
        Calls The Evans Country a "skilled and spirited sequence."

1963

9   DeMOTT, BENJAMIN. "Declining Civilization." <u>Harper's</u>, 227
     (July), 92-93.
        Review of <u>My Enemy's Enemy</u>. Amis is dazzled by democracy
     in this collection. "All the Blood Within Me" moves "beyond
     the simplicities of stern egalitarianism, and the results
     are striking."

10   DEMPSEY, DAVID. "Bucking the System." <u>The New York Times
     Book Review</u> (28 April), pp. 4, 48.
        Review of <u>My Enemy's Enemy</u>. Sees a combination of the
     serious and the "impish" sides of Amis here. It is too bad
     the first three stories on the military were not made into
     a novel, for they could have resulted in a revealing study
     of British military life. They reveal Amis to be "an astute
     critic who need not always be transparently funny." In
     them, the heroes learn that "bad manners--even immorality--
     is a justifiable means of maintaining one's position and
     self-respect." "All the Blood Within Me" is quite atypical
     of Amis. In it, he deals comfortably with ordinary people
     on straightforward terms.

11   DOLBIER, MAURICE. "Science-Fiction: 2 Stands for Zombie."
     <u>New York Herald Tribune</u> (26 July), p. 13.
        Brief mention of <u>Spectrum II</u>. Except for Henry Kuttner's
     "Vintage Season," this is a weak and unpersuasive collection.

12   EVANS, ILLTUD. "Visiting Fireman." <u>Tablet</u>, 217 (16 November),
     1238.
        Review of <u>One Fat Englishman</u>. "Amis brilliantly conveys
     the impact of his patronising imperception on the world of
     faculty parties and barbecues by the lake." The religious
     dimension to Roger's state is new for Amis. "Roger's re-
     ligion is curiously unreal, not merely in the sense that it
     is not practised but because it is only externally seen:
     just another eccentricity, like the snuff and the taste in
     ties."

13   FALCK, NORMAN. "The Lyrical Man." <u>The Review</u>, no. 5 (Febru-
     ary), pp. 40-41.
        Review of <u>The Evans Country</u>. "The trouble with Amis'
     no-nonsense technique, this kind of furious fidelity, is
     that it rules out poetry from the start." All we find,
     "over and above the crude notation of scenery and events,
     is a more or less abstract set of attitudes (love is sex,
     women are sentimental, if only sentiment was all right,
     etc.) to be worked up into punch-lines."

1963

14   GAINES, ERVIN J. "New Books Appraised: Fiction." <u>Library</u>
        <u>Journal</u>, 88 (15 March), 1177.
            Review of <u>My Enemy's Enemy</u>. Concludes that these stories
        do Amis no particular credit, for they fail to hold the
        reader's attention.

15   GRUMBACH, DORIS. Review of <u>My Enemy's Enemy</u>. <u>The Critic</u>,
        22 (August), 84.
            Amis deals with obscure areas of interest in these
        stories. They are poorly resolved and difficult to
        understand.

16   HICKS, GRANVILLE. "No Time for Anger." <u>Saturday Review</u>, 46
        (6 April), 22-23.
            Review of <u>My Enemy's Enemy</u>. In the first three wartime
        stories, we can see the developmental stages of Jim Dixon
        and Garnet Bowen. But as a whole, the short story is not
        Amis' forte. To begin with, Amis seems to have more to say
        than the form will allow. They lack the farce, the comedy,
        enjoyed in the novels. However, they do reveal something
        about his outlook on life--that he is a comic with a funda-
        mental seriousness, and that as an acute observer, there
        are distasteful and ridiculous things in modern life he
        chooses to laugh at. Thus, he avoids complacency and
        despair.

*17   HINGLEY, RONALD. "Soviet 'guide' to English Novels." London
        <u>Sunday Times</u> (3 February), p. 2.
            Unlocatable. Listed incorrectly in 1976.A1.

18   HOLLOWAY, DAVID. "Mr. Amis Prowls the Campus." London <u>Daily</u>
        <u>Telegraph</u> (15 November), p. 21.
            With <u>One Fat Englishman</u>, it is obvious Amis is "growing
        progressively less gamesome." Roger's misadventures are
        only a framework for Amis' mockery of campus life.

19   LODGE, DAVID. "The Modern, the Contemporary, and the Impor-
        tance of Being Amis." <u>Critical Quarterly</u>, 5 (Winter),
        340-354.
            Considers Amis in light of Spender's distinction be-
        tween the "modern" and the "contemporary." (<u>See</u> 1962.B32.)
        Although Amis rejects the modern mode, he is important be-
        cause of his use of language, his awareness of his limits,
        and his "sardonic" sense of literature. Close examination
        of <u>Lucky Jim</u> and <u>Take A Girl Like You</u> to illustrate these
        points. Reprint: 1966.B40.

20   MacCAIG, NORMAN. "Cygnets and Snow." The New Statesman, 65
     (22 February), 276.
         Review of The Evans Country. Amis comically exposes
     the truth behind human nature and deflates pretensions.

21   MARWICK, ARTHUR. "The Decade of Disenchantment," in his The
     Explosion of British Society: 1914-1962. London: Pan
     Books, p. 143.
         Finds several similarities between Charles Lumley (Wain's
     Hurry on Down) and Jim Dixon and John Lewis. "Beyond making
     explicit the dilemmas of the angry young man, these impor-
     tant novels breathe the atmosphere of a whole social mal-
     aise: covetousness."

22   MOBERG, GEORGE. "Structure and Theme in Amis's Novels." CEA
     Critic, 25 (March), 7, 10.
         Examines Amis' first four novels for structure and theme.
     Beginning with That Uncertain Feeling, Amis is a poor plot-
     maker. He avoids complexities of expression, and emphasizes
     rationality and candor. As a pessimist, humor makes life
     bearable in his novels.

23   NEMEROV, HOWARD. "Young Poets: The Lyric Difficulty," in his
     Poetry and Fiction Essays. New Brunswick: Rutgers Univer-
     sity Press, pp. 215-225.
         Reprint of 1958.B36. Excerpted: 1974.B33.

24   O'CONNOR, WILLIAM VAN. "Kingsley Amis," in his The New Uni-
     versity Wits and the End of Modernism. Carbondale: South-
     ern Illinois University Press, pp. 14, 33, 75-102.
         Amis is a satirist, not an angry man. In his criticism
     and his fiction he hits at pretentiousness in any form.
     Sees an anti-romantic bias and an appeal to common sense in
     Amis' critical theories, fiction and poetry. His novels
     don't have at the center any very profound searching out of
     psychological or philosophical principles, nor do they take
     a stand on class conflict. Although alternative values to
     affectations of the genteel and pretentious are implied,
     they are insufficiently explored. Includes some biographi-
     cal details and a selective bibliography of primary and
     secondary sources. Excerpted: 1973.B47.

25   POORE, CHARLES. "Books of The Times." New York Times (27
     April), p. 23.
         Review of My Enemy's Enemy. Amis shares his military
     experiences and shows how wartime attitudes of servility or
     defiance carry over into civilian life and vice versa. Ex-
     ploits the special caste system in wildly funny satire in

1963

the first three stories, and shows how many different things the same event may mean to different people. In the latter stories, human nature doesn't alter, even out of uniform.

26 POSTER, CONSTANCE. "Lucky Jim Grows Up." New Leader, 46 (27 May), 26-27.
Sees an Amis hero emerge from the first four novels and the short stories. In Jim Dixon, we see the negative anger of an adolescent. In That Uncertain Feeling, the hero has become more aware of feelings, and in Take A Girl Like You, Julian Ormerod exemplifies wasted potentiality.

27 POWELL, ANTHONY. "Kingsley's Heroes." The Spectator, 211 (29 November), 709-710.
Although Amis has a strong public personality, it is difficult to gauge the mood his name is associated with in the public's mind. Perhaps this is because Amis does not ascribe to any one particular theory; rather, his interest is in human beings. One Fat Englishman is a lively, enjoyable book. Although Micheldene seems to be an unpleasant character, Amis seems to have some sympathy for the man. There is some uncertainty just how horrible he actually is. Sees Lucky Jim as Amis' best novel. Take A Girl Like You is weak because of the technical difficulty of being told from a woman's point of view.

28 PRESS, JOHN. "Provincialism and Tradition," in his Rule and Energy: Trends in British Poetry Since the Second World War. London: Oxford University Press, pp. 92-97.
Notes that Amis is a provincial poet, concerned primarily with values of his own cultural society. Amis values feeling, fidelity to truth, originality, and sincerity. He is a highly literate poet, serious in his pronouncements against sham. Many of his clever poems are trivial, however.

29 PRITCHETT, V.S. "The Prognosticators." New Statesman, 66 (20 September), 360.
Brief mention of Spectrum III.

30 QUINN, MIRIAM. "Fiction." Best Sellers, 23 (15 May), 76-77.
Review of My Enemy's Enemy. These stories reveal Amis' obviously serious side. In "I Spy Strangers," we see Amis' sympathy with the common man. "All the Blood Within Me" is unique to Amis, for it is a "sensitive and touching study of a man who attends the funeral of a woman he has loved for years and of the unrecognized things he is forced to learn about the both of them."

31 RATCLIFFE, MICHAEL. "Amis in the thirteen colonies." London
      Sunday Times (17 November), p. 35.
          Review of One Fat Englishman. This is Amis' letter of
      "love-hate" to America. Amis observes characters at social
      gatherings, "where they are at the extremities of human be-
      haviour." Unfortunately, there is little detail to the
      novel and Amis imperfectly explains behaviour.

32 RICKS, CHRISTOPHER. "Cant Trap." New Statesman, 66 (29 No-
      vember), 790-792.
          Notes that Amis' heroes have grown progressively nastier.
      In One Fat Englishman, Amis seems to be trying to dissociate
      himself from Micheldene, and yet, in the end, he seems to
      like his hero. This is a technical problem. The book is
      more of a trap and less a novel, for in reacting to it we
      reveal our own prejudices. Lastly, it is really too short
      to develop the characters in any detail.

33 ROSS, MAGGIE. "New Novels." The Listener, 70 (21 November),
      852-853.
          Review of One Fat Englishman. There are "more smiles
      than laughs" in this novel. The only two noteworthy char-
      acters are Joe and Micheldene. Roger should have been
      given "a more substantial background to his affairs."

34 SALE, ROGER. "The Death of Science Fiction." Hudson Review,
      16 (Autumn), 475-476.
          Review of Spectrum II. Calls this a "weak collection."
      Refers to New Maps of Hell as a book lacking enthusiasm.
      "It is not that he loves science fiction less, but that he
      hates totalitarianism more."

35 TRACY, HONOR. "Fish out of Water." New Republic, 148 (1 June),
      23-24.
          Review of My Enemy's Enemy. The stories are slow and
      slack; Amis is better off writing novels. "All the Blood
      Within Me" is his best for its insights into the all-too-
      true aches and pains of a funeral.

36 WALDHORN, ARTHUR. "Mr. Amis Turns to the Short Story, But
      Perhaps Not for Long." The New York Herald Tribune Book
      Review (28 April), p. 4.
          Review of My Enemy's Enemy. Amis' satire is "brassy,
      and the effect, occasionally, leaden." Praises "Moral
      Fibre" for its "hilarious plotting and witty phrasing."

37 WEIGHTMAN, JOHN. "Mr. Amis goes metaphysical." The Observer
      (17 November), p. 24.

1963

Review of <u>One Fat Englishman</u>. Roger is the same "drunken, irascible lecher" we have seen earlier, only this time he has a metaphysical concern. This is the first novel "to be fully conceived as a tragi-comedy without sentimental over-tones, and therefore...the first one to be entirely success-ful within its own terms of reference."

38   WOOD, FREDERICK T. "Current Literature 1962." <u>English Studies</u>, 44 (June), 225.
     Review of <u>My Enemy's Enemy</u>. This is a study of people Amis dislikes. Each individual has "his own inner enemy in a particular side of his character which is in conflict with the kind of person he would like to be."

39   YOUNG, B.A. "Space-Time," <u>Punch</u>, 245 (2 October), 507.
     Brief mention of <u>Spectrum III</u>.

<u>1964 A BOOKS - NONE</u>

<u>1964 B SHORTER WRITINGS</u>

1   AGIUS, AMBROSE. "Fiction." <u>Best Sellers</u>, 23 (1 March), 409-410.
     Review of <u>One Fat Englishman</u>. Comments on Amis' pene-trating eye for character and the American scene. Like Juvenal and some of Waugh, Amis stresses vice rather than normality. Unlike Juvenal, Amis "exposes the frightful boredom of anti-social vice in a way that recalls the hell of ennui described by C.S. Lewis." Amis has a "salty wit."

2   ALLEN, WALTER. "War and Post War: British," in his <u>The Mod-ern Novel in Britain and the United States</u>. New York: Dutton, pp. 278-282.
     Reprint of 1964.B3. Excerpted: 1966.B60; 1973.B47.

3   _____. "War and Post War: British," in his <u>Tradition and Dream: The English and American Novel from the 1920's to Our Time</u>. London: Phoenix House, pp. 278-282.
     Jim Dixon has become an archetypal figure. The clue to Amis' point of view in <u>I Like It Here</u> is the passage on Henry Fielding. Notes that the element of moral seriousness becomes increasingly evident in his later novels. Amis' development as a moralist is straightforward. Reprint: 1962.B2. Excerpted: 1966.B60; 1973.B47.

4   ALLSOP, KENNETH. "The Neutralists," in his <u>The Angry Decade: A Survey of the Cultural Revolt of the Nineteen-Fifties</u>.

London: Peter Owen, pp. 43-58.
Amis' "disenchanted low browism" runs through his work.
He has been misrepresented by critics. The comedy is most
important in <u>Lucky Jim</u>. Excerpted: 1966.B60.

5   ANON. "Beastly Business." <u>Time</u>, 83 (21 February), 96.
Review of <u>One Fat Englishman</u>. Amis' aim is serious comedy in this novel. Micheldene is a pathetic as well as de-
testable character whom we pity at the end. Comments on the
mimic's ear for American dialogue in the novel.

6   ANON. "Old Budweiser." <u>Newsweek</u>, 63 (2 March), 86-87.
Sees <u>One Fat Englishman</u> as a satire on Princeton University. Says the prose is direct, reflecting "the untrammeled
<u>angst</u> that distinguishes his <u>Lucky Jim</u>." Does find some
flaws in the American dialogue, however. Includes a brief
interview in which Amis tells of his other interests.

7   ANON. "Construing The 1963 Act." London <u>Times</u> (7 May), p. 8.
Brief biographical entry. James Maxwell Douglas-Henry
given divorce from Elizabeth Jane Douglas-Henry because of
adultery with Amis.

8   BALDANZA, FRANK. <u>Ivy Compton-Burnett</u>. Twayne English Authors
Series, edited by Sylvia E. Bowman. Boston: Twayne Publishers, pp. 107, 126-138.
As a realist, Amis feels that Compton Burnett's characters are diffuse, that her plots are melodramatic and arbi-
trary, that her dialogue is artificial, and that her world
is lacking progress, change, or improvement. Notes that
Amis' objections stem from a lack of sympathy, for Compton
Burnett does these things as only she can. Amis does feel
her sense of the comic saves her, and he admires her for
her hatred of tyranny and her pity for the victim.

9   BARRETT, WILLIAM. "Angry Englishman." <u>The Atlantic Monthly</u>,
213 (April), 144-145.
Review of <u>One Fat Englishman</u>. Excellent for the violent
satire and the buffoonery of its characters.

10   BERGONZI, BERNARD. "Reputations--IX: Kingsley Amis." <u>London
Magazine</u>, NS 4 (January), 50-65.
Amis is more than a comic writer, for he and his characters become grimmer in later novels. The poetry in <u>A Frame
of Mind</u> hints at his other interests. Notes, for example,
a careful verbal finish and a "brooding concern" with death
and sex. "Against Romanticism" presents a world without
myth. Sees a purely anti-romantic vision which carries over

1964

into his novels. This is basically a Hobbesian world in
which Amis is determined to make every detail meaningful.
Notes a prominence of cruel, even sadistic, fantasy in the
novels. Assesses Amis' first five novels and concludes that
Take A Girl Like You is unsuccessful because Amis fails to
justify its long length. It is marked by "moral incoherence"
and "an authorial ambivalence." Partially reprinted in
1970.B7.

11   BROPHY, BRIGID. "Just Jim." London Sunday Times Magazine (26
January), pp. 11-13.
    In retrospect, feels Amis keeps rewriting the same novel.
The only development is that his heroes become nastier.
Amis is an ambiguous moralist as he moves from whimsicality
to passing moral judgment. Comments on Amis' facetious
style and farce of situation. Reprinted: 1966.B13. Excerpted: 1973.B33.

12   BUITENHUIS, PETER. "An Appetite for Booze and Helene." The
New York Tribune Book Review (1 March), p. 5.
    Review of One Fat Englishman. Questions how coherent
and convincing Micheldene is, and says the novel is too
short and too much a part of the comic-realist school of
British fiction to contain the existential dilemma of Roger.
Notes that Roger is the only total charcter in the novel;
the others are mere caricatures.

13   DEGNAN, J.P. "Scourge of the Establishment." Commonweal, 80
(19 June), 402-403.
    Review of One Fat Englishman. Unlike his earlier novels,
this one is ambiguous, for it is unclear what Amis is sati-
rizing or what the characters typify. Says the farce is
entertaining, however.

14   DeMOTT, BENJAMIN. "Of Snobs and Taxes and Unimpressed Men."
Harper's Magazine, 228 (April), 106-107.
    Review of One Fat Englishman. A new departure for Amis.
It is a book on snobbery, but almost for the first time,
the point of view character is the snob. Concludes that
the comedy interrupts what might be a serious study into
the source of human misery.

15   FRASER, GEORGE SUTHERLAND. The Modern Writer and His World.
London: Deutsch, pp. 169-179, 346-348.
    Notes the "penetrating realism" in Lucky Jim. Dixon is
a male Cinderella, a "put-upon man." Comments on the imbal-
ance between seriousness, farce and high comedy in That Uncertain Feeling, but also notes that Amis is at the top of

his form with new themes in this novel. Sees parallels between Amis and Henry Fielding, and discusses Amis' association with the poetic Movement. Reprinted: 1964.B16.

16 _____. The Modern Writer and His World. Baltimore: Penguin Books, pp. 176-179, 346-348.
Reprint of 1964.B15.

17 FURBANK, P.N. "Western Approaches." Encounter, 22 (January), 76.
Review of One Fat Englishman. Amis is a didactic writer who retreats to one of the basic forms of English fiction in this novel; that is, he "prepares hero for, and then exposes him to, an ethical crisis, leaving him thereafter on the path to salvation or damnation."

18 GARDINER, HAROLD C. "One Crashing Bore." America, 110 (11 April), 515.
Review of One Fat Englishman. Although intended to be funny, Amis doesn't succeed. It is totally unconvincing that Roger could capture the affections of the ladies, or that the priest should be so fatuous. There is little satire here.

19 GENTHE, CHARLES V. "What Price Academe? Or, Kingsley Amis Revisited." Satire Newsletter, 2 (Spring), 44.
A parody of Amis' tropes in Lucky Jim.

20 GRIFFINS, JOHN. "Paperback SF." London Sunday Times (20 December), p. 16.
Brief mention of Spectrum III.

21 HAMILTON, KENNETH. "Kingsley Amis, Moralist." Dalhousie Review, 44 (Autumn), 339-347.
Examines Amis' novels through One Fat Englishman and three stories in My Enemy's Enemy. Notes an underlying consistency of moral judgment, that of the revenge of the underprivileged against those privileged who seem immune to such attacks. The "interaction between class and power is the center of his moral concern." Concludes by saying Amis is a "guardian of the puritan conscience."

22 HARTLEY, ANTHONY. "Everyman in America." New Leader, 47 (27 April), 26-27.
Review of One Fat Englishman and a reassessment of Amis. It has been Amis' "fate to have the social significance side of his writing emphasized at the expense of the more personal themes which run throughout his novels." Amis is more

1964

than a novelist of social observations. Jim Dixon, for example, is Everyman in the modern world facing "obstructive
bureaucracy." The solution to this, for Amis, is humor.
What is essential is the free mind, and Dixon manages to
assert his individuality and free himself from social ties.
In That Uncertain Feeling, Lewis and his wife lack conventions. Everything is out in the open, and this works de-
structively against them. The theme of breakdown of
conventions is carried further in Take A Girl Like You.
Notes less optimism here. There are more broken-down fig-
ures, and the world is soured with a minimum of happiness.
No longer are his heroes masters of their environment; now
they are enslaved by it. In One Fat Englishman, Amis com-
pletes the study into the failure of his hero's control of
circumstances begun in Lucky Jim. Roger fails to understand
the world around him. He is objectionable because he dis-
regards all conventions and feelings.

23   HOYT, C.A. "Pans Across the Sea." Saturday Review, 47 (7
     March), 38-39.
          Brief review of One Fat Englishman. Not an overwhelm-
     ingly funny novel. Finds some difficulty with trying to
     satirize both Americans and Englishmen at the same time.

24   JONES, D.A.N. "Amis's English Usage." New York Review of
     Books, 2 (April), 13-15.
          Review of One Fat Englishman. As an upper-class, thor-
     oughly discreditable Englishman, Micheldene's function is
     to be tormented. This reflects a prevailing mood in England.
     Micheldene differs from previous Amis heroes in that he is
     more like one of Amis' villains. He feels his social status
     protects him. Concludes by showing how Amis contrasts
     England and America in the language of the novel.

25   LARKIN, PHILIP. "Introduction," in his Jill. New York: St.
     Martin's Press, pp. 15-18.
          Memoir of Amis' college days. Notes that Amis was dis-
     tinguished chiefly by a "genius for imaginative mimicry"
     which he often used as the quickest way of convincing some-
     one that "something was horrible or boring or absurd." On
     the serious side, Amis was interested in politics. He suf-
     fered the familiar humorist's fate, however, of being unable
     to get anyone to take him seriously at times. Also mentions
     Amis' intense interest in jazz.

26   LEJEUNE, ANTHONY. "Worlds Enough And Time." Tablet, 218 (4
     January), 13-14.
          Review of Spectrum III. This collection contains one

story "which is simple adventure, one which is simply in-
comprehensible and one which is a joke: but almost all its
stories start from genuine, speculative ideas." Finds that
Amis feels "science fiction provokes critical thought about
the present by extending our current sociological and technical experience to points of absurdity, horror or
wonderment."

27   LEVINE, PAUL. "Individualism and the Traditional Talent."
     Hudson Review, 17 (Autumn), 470–471.
         Review of One Fat Englishman. Amis turns traditional
     comedy into new satire on foreign relations, with Roger ex-
     hibiting "the worst of merrie England." One Fat Englishman
     is Lucky Jim in reverse.

28   MADDOCKS, MELVIN. "When the Offbeat Goes Glib." Christian
     Science Monitor (19 March), p. 9.
         Despite his stylishness, Amis' satire doesn't entirely
     succeed because he must see everything as either a funny or
     a dirty story. In One Fat Englishman, a more serious novel
     is trying to be released from a farce. Roger is Jim Dixon
     in exile. Amis seems fearful of meaning, for he is troubled
     by doubts about his nihilism and unwilling to admit life is
     better.

29   MOON, ERIC. "New Books Appraised: Fiction." Library Journal,
     89 (15 February), 880.
         Brief review of One Fat Englishman. Amis' best work
     since That Uncertain Feeling. This is a satire on American
     life and snobbish Englishmen, in which Amis seems to imply
     sympathy for the hero. Says we end up liking the author
     less than the characters.

30   O'CONNOR, WILLIAM VAN. "Parody As Criticism." College English,
     25 (January), 247–248.
         Studies the parody of Dylan Thomas and T.S. Eliot in
     That Uncertain Feeling. This is good-humored satire, for
     "we allow ourselves to be taken in by arty poses."

31   PANTER-DOWNES, MOLLIE. "That Certain Missing Feeling." The
     New Yorker, 40 (June), 134–136.
         Review of One Fat Englishman. A totally believable nov-
     el, for it lacks the touch of affection for characters Amis
     has shown in his earlier novels. There is so much nasti-
     ness and disgust in Roger's character, it is hard to feel
     any sympathy for him. Thus, his tears at the end fail to
     touch the reader.

1964

32 PRESCOTT, ORVILLE. "The Awful Mr. Micheldene and Other Mon-
        sters." New York Times (26 February), p. 33.
            Review of One Fat Englishman. Clever and witty but un-
        funny and dull. Amis mixes contempt and sympathy for Roger,
        who is so offensive he seems more of a caricature. The
        same holds true for the other characters. The novel "con-
        tains numerous imaginative twists of plot, numerous patches
        of rather surprising dialogue and no real evidence that
        Kingsley Amis is very mad at anybody."

33 RICHARDSON, MAURICE. "Back to the bad old days." The Observer
        (3 May), p. 25.
            Review of A Question About Hell, Amis' television play,
        after it appeared on BBC. The play is obviously a refer-
        ence to The Duchess of Malfi, "with a modern West Indian
        setting with a miscegenation plot leading up to a pile of
        corpses." Calls it "a legitimate exercise that didn't
        succeed."

34 SHEED, WILFRED. "A Blustering Bundle Sent to Annoy Us." The
        New York Herald Tribune Book Week (1 March), p. 4.
            Review of One Fat Englishman. A sly commentary on
        America, using Roger, a stock comic character, to make some
        sour and original points. Amis bounces things off Roger,
        who is "alternately blind and immensely shrewd, and who re-
        veals things now by seeing them and now by not."

35 SKLAR, ROBERT. "Lots of Yaks In Oxbridge." Reporter, 31 (16
        July), 47.
            Review of One Fat Englishman. Amis' later heroes be-
        come more obsessed with sex and more complacent with their
        lot, all of which reveals "the juvenile cast of mind"
        among Amis' heroes. In One Fat Englishman, this trend is
        carried to the extreme. Roger is unlike the earlier heroes
        except for his obsession with sex.

36 SOULE, GEORGE. "The High Cost of Plunging." Carleton Miscel-
        lany, 5 (Fall), 106-111.
            Review of One Fat Englishman. Amis is a mature novelist
        now, for he has progressed from a lightweight satirist and
        entertainer to a novelist of stature. He has located the
        roots of human misery in the heart of Roger, whose fatness
        is symbolic of "an inward and spiritual corruption." Anger
        is his undoing. He is an upper-class snob Amis has always
        detested. We pity and hate him. And yet, One Fat English-
        man does not succeed because its characters (except for
        Roger and Molly) are contrived, lifeless and unbelievable,
        and its dialogue is undistinguished. Amis tries to be

profound, significant and funny, but he fails. All things
considered, <u>Lucky Jim</u> is still Amis' best novel because it
was a new kind of novel and because all of its elements were
created "from the same impulse."

37   WARD, ANTHONY. "Jimsday." <u>The Spectator</u>, 212 (27 January),
     112.
          Calls <u>That Uncertain Feeling</u> the best of Amis' first five
     novels. Despite all of the paraded funniness and mannerism,
     there is still something authentic in Amis. Divides Amis'
     characters into two categories: aggressive phonies unaware
     of their phoniness, and defensive but self-aware phonies.

38   WIGGIN, MAURICE. "Miscegenation à la Mode." London <u>Sunday</u>
     <u>Times</u> (3 May), p. 32.
          Review of Amis' television play on BBC, <u>A Question About</u>
     <u>Hell</u>. It is "melodramatic" and "unbelievable." Amis might
     be saying something about "the correlation of racial and
     sexual prejudices."

39   WOOD, F.T. "Current Literature: 1963." <u>English Studies</u>, 45
     (June), 260-261.
          Review of <u>One Fat Englishman</u>. Views this as "a satire
     on the vulgarity, bad taste and snobbishness of a certain
     type of Englishman who imagines that he is a good ambassa-
     dor for his country when all the time he is creating the
     worst of impressions and making himself look either foolish
     or objectionable." Notes a return to Amis' earlier style
     of writing with this novel.

1965 A BOOKS

1   SMITH, ROBERT BRUCE. "An Analysis of the Novels of Kingsley
     Amis." Ph. D. dissertation, University of Washington.
          Detailed analysis of Amis' first five novels. Examines
     his comedy and his development as a novelist. Notes a
     growing self-knowledge, an acute observation of the charac-
     ter's experience, and an increase in skill as a technician.

1965 B SHORTER WRITINGS

1   ADAMS, PHOEBE. "Potpourri." <u>The Atlantic Monthly</u>, 216 (July),
     144.
          Review of <u>The James Bond Dossier</u>. An entertaining but
     not entirely serious study filled with many "shrewd
     insights."

1965

2   ANON. "Law Report, March 5." London <u>Times</u> (6 March), p. 18.
        Brief biographical report on Amis.

3   ANON. "Fiction." <u>Saturday Review</u>, 48 (20 March), 33.
        Brief review of <u>One Fat Englishman</u>. Calls the novel a
     "funny account."

4   ANON. "Non-fiction." <u>Kirkus</u>, 33 (15 May), 513.
        Review of <u>The James Bond Dossier</u>. Calls this an "enter-
     taining exegesis of the compleat Bond for the compleat col-
     lector thereof."

5   ANON. "An Englishman's Bond." <u>The Times Literary Supplement</u>
     (27 May), p. 408.
        Review of <u>The James Bond Dossier</u>. A well-written, witty,
     expert dossier. Summary of contents.
        Reprinted: 1966.B1.

6   ANON. Review of <u>The James Bond Dossier</u>. <u>Choice</u>, 2 (June),
     207.
        Brief mention. Says Amis sees Bond as a twentieth cen-
     tury hero.

7   ANON. "Style Out In Space." <u>The Times Literary Supplement</u>
     (10 June), p. 469.
        Brief mention of <u>Spectrum IV</u>.

8   ANON. "Way Down--Way Out." <u>Kirkus</u>, 33 (1 July), 653.
        Brief review of <u>Spectrum IV</u>. Contains "mostly marvelous
     stories."

9   ANON. "Lit." <u>Booklist</u>, 61 (15 July), 1048.
        Brief mention of <u>The James Bond Dossier</u>. Calls it a
     "highly readable commentary."

10   ANON. "Notes on Current Books." <u>Virginia Quarterly Review</u>,
     41 (Autumn), cxlviii.
        Brief mention of <u>The James Bond Dossier</u>. Amis defends
     Bond with "wit and charm."

11   ANON. "New Fiction." London <u>Times</u> (14 October), p. 15.
        Review of <u>The Egyptologists</u>. A good romp without any
     supremely funny moments. It relates to Amis' canon, who is
     known for debunking academe.

12   ANON. "Shy Society." <u>The Times Literary Supplement</u> (14 Octo-
     ber), p. 913.

Review of The Egyptologists. A stale, unfunny study of "deception as an art."

13 ANON. "Quick Looks." London Evening Standard (26 October), p. 19.
Brief mention of The Egyptologists. Summarizes the plot and comments on the funny scenes.

14 ANON. "Short reports." London Sunday Times (31 October), p. 53.
Review of The Egyptologists. A comedy of manners in the "'Cold Comfort Farm'" idiom. Although a bit too long, the plot devices are ingenious and the writing is bright.

15 ANON. "Books Received." The Times Literary Supplement, (18 November), p. 1029.
Brief reference to Amis on the dust jacket of William Tanner's The Book of Bond.

16 BOARDMAN, TOM. "Science Fiction: Tom Boardman praises the iconoclast." Books & Bookmen, 10 (May), 34.
Brief mention of Spectrum IV. This is an "impeccable selection" with the accent on sociological speculation.

17 BOWEN, JOHN. "Unhappy division." London Sunday Times (4 April), p. 32.
Brief mention of Spectrum IV and summary of contents.

18 BRITTON, ANNE. "and another view of the fictional secret service." Books & Bookmen, 10 (July), 10-11.
Review of The James Bond Dossier. Notes that Amis' interest is aroused by Bond's and M's social standing. Calls this a complete study with meticulous observations.

19 BROOKE, JOCELYN. "New fiction." The Listener, 74 (28 October), 677.
Review of The Egyptologists. A dull and humdrum novel with an unnecessarily over-complicated plot. The first two chapters remind him of G.K. Chesterton's The Man Who Was Thursday.

20 BURGESS, ANTHONY. "Sins of Simony." The Spectator, 215 (15 October), 491-492.
Review of The Egyptologists. Calls it "a good and funny book."

21 CAMPBELL, ALEX. "Thrillers for Eggheads." New Republic, 153 (3 July), 25-26.

1965

Brief mention of The James Bond Dossier. Amis attempts
to show that James Bond is more than just fun.

22   CAPLAN, RALPH. "Kingsley Amis," in Contemporary British Nov-
      elists. Edited by Charles Shapiro. Carbondale: Southern
      Illinois University Press, pp. 3-15.
         A general survey of Amis' first five novels. Says the
      reader oversimplifies Amis if he focuses only on what he
      says; rather, he must look at how Amis says it. For in-
      stance, the most interesting sexual relationships are un-
      consummated or inactive because of the descriptions of his
      characters' fantasies. Moreover, Amis uses anger as "an
      instrument of revelation and self-revelation." He is also
      rather old-fashioned in that his characters are exaggerated
      into believability, they are surrounded by credible minor
      characters, and the plot follows conventional lines. Finds
      that affectation is Amis' most amusing enemy. Excerpted:
      1973.B47.

23   CONQUEST, ROBERT. "Christian Symbolism in Lucky Jim." Criti-
      cal Quarterly, 7 (June), 87-92.
         A parody in which Conquest views Lucky Jim as a World
      Fable and finds a pervasive tone of religious symbolism in
      the verbal level and the basic structure of the novel.
      Dixon is both Everyman and the Son of Man. The plot is the
      universal conflict between the powers of darkness and light.

24   CUFF, SERGEANT. "Criminal Record." Saturday Review, 48 (26
      June), 34.
         Brief mention of The James Bond Dossier which he calls
      "admiring, analytical, and informative."

25   DICKINSON, PETER. "007." Punch, 249 (14 July), 67.
         Brief mention of The James Bond Dossier, which he calls
      "a cool and intelligent defence."

26   EWART, GAVIN. "Bondage." The London Magazine, NS 5 (June),
      92-96.
         Review of The James Bond Dossier. A thorough, entertain-
      ing and serious study. Focuses on Amis' comments on adven-
      ture, Bond's personality, jargon, sex, sadism, brand names
      and patriotism.

27   GRANT, M.K. "New Books Appraised: Lit." Library Journal, 90
      (15 June), 2855.
         Review of The James Bond Dossier. An entertaining book
      covering "the life and times of the folk hero...and the psy-
      chology and intellect of those who disapprove of him."

28   HALL, STUART. "A Question of Tone." Manchester Guardian (4
      June), p. 9.
            Review of The James Bond Dossier. Amis identifies
      Fleming's weaknesses and strengths. He clearly delineates
      the basic elements in the Bond cycle and gives insight into
      Fleming's qualities as a writer. Amis' judgments are mud-
      dled, however, when he identifies the moral framework in
      Fleming. Reprinted: 1965.B29.

29   _____. "The world of 007." Manchester Guardian Weekly, 92
      (10 June), 11.
            Reprint of 1965.B28.

30   HIGGINS, JOHN. "Daddies and Mummies." London Sun Telegraph
      (17 October), p. 13.
            Brief mention of The Egyptologists.

31   HINE, AL. "What Have They Done to Our Hero?" The New York
      Times Book Review (25 July), p. 4.
            Review of The James Bond Dossier. Amis reveals his "pu-
      ritan conscience" in a study which is too late and is a
      foolish and fatal extension philosophically. Obviously,
      Amis doesn't wish us to enjoy Bond for what he is.

32   HOPKINS, KENNETH. "Fiction: Kenneth Hopkins on a whimpering
      spoof." Books & Bookmen, 11 (December), 42.
            Review of Colonel Sun. Calls this a "weak, immature and
      outrageously unentertaining book."

33   JACOB, ALARIC. "From Pop to Pop." London Sunday Times (30
      May), p. 26.
            Review of The James Bond Dossier. Amis defends Fleming
      against charges of snobbery and sadism, and is captivated
      by Fleming's skill as an entertainer. The study is weak,
      however, for although Amis knows Bond, he doesn't seem to
      know Fleming. Says Fleming fulfilled his talent as a de-
      scriptive journalist and travel writer. He knew he wasn't
      a serious writer.

34   JONES, D.A.N. "Bondage." The New York Review of Books (14
      October), pp. 18, 27.
            Says The James Bond Dossier has little to do with the
      ability of Fleming.

35   KATONA, ANNA. "The Decline of the Modern in Recent British
      Fiction." Zeitschriftür Anglistik und Amerikanistik, 13,
      (Winter), pp. 35-44.

1965

Distinguishes between Amis' generation and James Joyce's. See also 1962.B32 and 1963.B19.

36   KAUFFMAN, STANLEY. "Literature of the Early Sixties." Wilson Library Bulletin, 39 (May), 763.
Review of One Fat Englishman. The most serious fault in this novel is that it is hard to tell whether Amis is aware that while held up for ridicule, Roger triumphs at the end. "It is funny, but most of the time it is funny in the manner of the practical entertainer who knows he has been laughed at in the past and is depending to some extent on his reputation for humor."

37   LEJEUNE, ANTHONY. "Amis On Bond." Tablet, 219 (29 May), 607-608.
Review of The James Bond Dossier. This study tells us nothing new about Bond and very little about Amis. Criticizes Amis' lack of incisive comments on the Blades Club, Bond's food and drink, and external evidence about Bond.

38   "MANDRAKE" [JOHN SUMMERS]. "ADL." London Sunday Telegraph (14 February), p. 13.
Interview in which Amis comments on the writing of The Anti-Death League.

39   MAYNE, RICHARD. "Gentlemen Prefer Bonds." New Statesman, 69 (4 June), 883-884.
Short review of The James Bond Dossier. Agrees with Amis that there is an intellectual cult around Bond. Disagrees with some points of Amis' defense by saying one can always find reprehensible elements in popular fiction. Says fantasy is therapeutic in Bond.

40   MILLER, WARREN. "Books." Commonweal, 82 (6 August), 569-570.
Review of The James Bond Dossier. Says Amis is "eulogizing and touting mediocrity." A silly, unimportant book, marked by a bad style.

41   MONTGOMERY, JOHN. "Young? Angry? Typical?" Books & Bookmen, 11 (December), 86-87.
A history of Lucky Jim's success, tracing the story from both Amis' and his publisher's points of view.

42   MORAL, E. "A Russian Elite." New Statesman, 69 (14 May), 772.
Brief favorable mention of Spectrum IV.

43   MUGGERIDGE, MALCOLM. "James Bond: Malcolm Muggeridge Examines The Myth And Its Master." The Observer (30 May), p. 21.

Review of <u>The James Bond Dossier</u>. Bond is both a social
and literary phenomenon and deserves the "meticulous attention" Amis gives to him. Admires his analysis of "M."

44 _____. Review of <u>The James Bond Dossier</u>. <u>Critic</u>, 24 (October-
November), 64.
This study may come in handy in academe. Says a compar-
ison by Amis of Fleming and Spillane would be interesting.

45 MURRAY, BRIAN J. "Non-Fiction." <u>Best Sellers</u>, 25 (15 July),
p. 175.
Review of <u>The James Bond Dossier</u>. The main function of
this study is that it acts as an "intellectual catharsis;"
that is, Amis examines Bond "as more than a mere cloak-and-
dagger man with absolutely no moral code." He shows how
Fleming couples the realistic with the unrealistic. Concludes that the book should be read for its scholarship.

46 PAUL, LESLIE. "The Angry Young Man Revisited." <u>Kenyon Review</u>,
27 (Spring), 344-352.
In explaining why <u>Lucky Jim</u> was successful, Paul finds
an intense social self-consciousness and general sexual
confusion in the novel. The later novels are not particu-
larly noteworthy. Amis never returns to the genius of his
first book.

47 POORE, CHARLES. "A Lively Inquiry Into James Bondolatry."
<u>The New York Times</u> (29 June), p. 33.
Review of <u>The James Bond Dossier</u>. Amis explains Bond as
a cultural folk hero and secret agent. He examines the fantasy and entertaining elements that appeal to readers.

48 PRICE, R.G.G. "New Novels." <u>Punch</u>, 249 (27 October), 625.
Brief mention of <u>The Egyptologists</u>. Says this is a book
more enjoyable than it should be.

49 PRYCE-JONES, ALAN. "An Admirer of James Bond." <u>New York Herald Tribune</u> (29 June), p. 21.
Brief mention of <u>The James Bond Dossier</u>.

50 RAVEN, SIMON. "Amis and the Eggheads." <u>The Spectator</u>, 262
(28 May), 694-695.
Review of <u>The James Bond Dossier</u>. Amis confutes several
charges against Bond and Fleming and makes some positive
points about Fleming as a writer. The thesis of the book
is actually "an onslaught on the more silly and pompous of
[Bond's and Fleming's] critics,...a vindication of the pro-
cesses...of rational common sense." So Amis attacks from

1965

a new angle all the targets he's attacked earlier in his
novels. This is, he concludes, "a mature, authoritative and
affectionate moral apologia."

51   REES, DAVID. "That Petrine Cock." The Spectator, 215 (27
     August), 268-269.
          That Uncertain Feeling is Amis' best novel because of
     the combination of humor, social observations and an un-
     equivocal attitude towards moral dilemmas. The comic inter-
     ludes are irrelevant to the main drive of the plot. Lewis'
     involvement with the Gruffydd-Williamses is particularly ef-
     fective. Lewis' integrity is based on a hostility toward
     cultural pretentiousness and an existential distrust of
     abstractions. The range of his experience is large.

52   REID, COLIN. "Wipe off the lipstick with your tie!" London
     Daily Mail (14 October), p. 8.
          Brief mention of The Egyptologists.

53   SEMPLE, JR., ROBERT B. "It's That Superman Again--Public Spy
     No. 1." The National Observer (27 December), p. 17.
          Review of The James Bond Dossier. An excellent book;
     Amis has done his homework. "He has read the books care-
     fully, thought about their popularity, and taken them seri-
     ously as cultural phenomena." Recommends Amis start
     reviewing some of the Bond movies.

54   SMITH, GENE. "Goldigger." New York Herald Tribune Book Week
     (29 August), pp. 1, 17.
          Review of The James Bond Dossier. He doesn't care for
     Bond and is at variance with Amis.

55   STEVENS, ELIZABETH. "Just What I Wanted!" Books & Bookmen,
     11 (December), 11-12.
          Brief mention of The James Bond Dossier with summary of
     its contents.

56   TAUBMAN, ROBERT. "Muddle." New Statesman, 70 (15 October),
     571-572.
          Review of The Egyptologists. In subject matter, this
     novel reflects the plight of males in a monogamous society,
     but it's still a dreary novel. The style is most pleasing,
     for the authors use Egyptology to "turn the academic mode
     against itself."

57   TREVOR, WILLIAM. "Comic-strip wonder." The Listener, 73 (27
     May), 788.
          Review of The James Bond Dossier. A valuable book to

Bond fans, but Amis fails to answer the question of why
Bond was so popular.

58   WARDLE, IRVING. "A Dublin Romance." The Observer (17 October),
        p. 28.
            Unfavorable review of The Egyptologists. Calls it "a
        heavy un-joke of stupefying unreadability" weighted down by
        obscure English literature gags and an over-complicated
        idea.

59   WHITE, GAVIN. "Bonded Stock." Canadian Forum, 45 (November),
        187-188.
            Review of The James Bond Dossier, which he calls "a se-
        rious study." Amis never really explains fully why the
        books sell, though he provides all the data. The best part
        is the reality of details in Fleming and his expertise on
        little points of reference.

60   WILSON, EDMUND. "Is It Possible to Pat Kingsley Amis?" The
        New Yorker, 32 (24 March), 140-147.
            Reprint of 1956.B21.

61   YOUNG, B.A. "Space-Time." Punch, 248 (7 April), 525.
            Brief mention of Spectrum IV. Calls it the best anthol-
        ogy of science fiction ever encountered.

1966 A BOOKS - NONE

1966 B SHORTER WRITINGS

1   ANON. "An Englishman's Bond," in Essays and Reviews from The
        Times Literary Supplement: 1965. Oxford and New York:
        Oxford University Press, pp. 120-125.
            Reprint of 1965.B6.

2   ANON. "Current & Various." Time, 87 (11 February), 94.
            Brief mention of The Egyptologists. Neither a funny nor
        a lively book.

3   ANON. "Beastly to God." The Times Literary Supplement (17
        March), p. 217.
            Review of The Anti-Death League. A somber book with a
        "strong air of protest," invigorated by the fact that the
        theme and style are at odds. It is a combination suspense
        novel, spy story, psychological thriller, science fiction
        novel and technical handbook "all mixed with a strong fla-
        vouring of double bluff."

1966

4   ANON. Review of <u>The Egyptologists</u>. <u>Choice</u>, 3 (May), 206.
     Notes "a certain pale ironical moral to this too-long
     comedy."

5   ANON. "Fiction." <u>Kirkus</u>, 34 (16 June), 598.
     Review of <u>The Anti-Death League</u>. A hard-to-follow "con-
     glomerate chronicle" using many techniques from parody to
     satire. Calls it "an intellectual thriller."

6   ANON. "Gloomy Recipe." <u>Newsweek</u>, 68 (22 August), 101.
     Review of <u>The Anti-Death League</u>. A boring mixture of
     "tedium and tumult"; the characters are "set-pieces."

7   ANON. "In Out of the Cold War." <u>Time</u>, 78 (26 August), 82.
     Review of <u>The Anti-Death League</u>. "An intelligent man's
     nightmare, with the famous Amis wit flickering an unkindly
     light amid the encircling gloom." Amis presents a "highly
     sophisticated and almost credible solution."

8   ANON. "Fiction." <u>Booklist</u>, 63 (1 November), 300.
     Favorable review of <u>The Anti-Death League</u>. "A complex,
     provocative novel, which can be enjoyed at several levels."

9   ANON. "Marius The Martian." <u>The Times Literary Supplement</u>
     (3 November), p. 1008.
     Brief mention of <u>The Anti-Death League</u>. This novel de-
     mands special physical and chemical knowledge by the reader
     to be understood.

10   BERGONZI, BERNARD. "Anything Goes." <u>The New York Review of
     Books</u> (6 October), p. 28.
     Ever since <u>Lucky Jim</u>, Amis' novels have grown steadily
     gloomier, until he plunges into the "dark side" in <u>The Anti-
     Death League</u>. This novel differs from the others in that
     it is flatter in tone, its point of view changes as the nar-
     rative develops, and it is symbolic fiction, a novel of
     ideas. Although the moral concerns don't mix very well with
     the thriller elements, we must respect Amis' seriousness
     and determination to write yet another different book, there-
     by avoiding self-imitation. Partially reprinted: 1966.B11.
     Excerpted: 1973.B33.

11   ____. "Selected Books." <u>The London Magazine</u>, NS 6 (June),
     109-112.
     Review of <u>The Anti-Death League</u>. This novel rounds off
     the first phase of Amis' career. In this, Amis is closer
     to symbolism than ever before; it is more generalized fic-
     tion. As a spy story, it reminds one of Deighton and

Le Carré. "Is a novel of ideas, whose theme is the inevita-
bility of death." As a novel of ideas, it is interesting
and provocative; as a novel, it is feeble and unconvincing.
Parts of this review come from 1966.B10.

12   BOARDMAN, TOM. "The Sky Is Not The Limit." Books & Bookmen,
     11 (March), 64-65.
        Brief mention of New Maps of Hell. Praises it for giving
     status to science fiction.

13   BROPHY, BRIGID. "Just Jim." London Sunday Times Magazine (26
     January), pp. 11-13.
        Reprint of 1964.B11. Excerpted: 1973.B33.

14   BROUN, HEYWOOD HALE. "Top Secrets and Cosmic Riddles." Sat-
     urday Review, 49 (20 August), 31.
        Review of The Anti-Death League. This novel has all of
     Amis' virtues--comedy, sex, good story--but on a larger
     scale than before. A vivid cast within a comic novel is
     used to make a deeply felt statement. This is an exciting
     development in Amis' career.

15   BURGESS, ANTHONY. "The Great Gangster." The Listener, 75 (17
     March), 401.
        Review of The Anti-Death League. Amis shows his serious
     side in this novel. Here, good must rest with man. In the
     early novels, laughter was a "palliative of hopelessness."
     Calls the novel a "masque of ultimate bitterness" against
     God.

16   BYATT, A.S. "Mess and Mystery." Encounter, 27 (July), 59-62.
        As a moralist, Amis must search for fact and reason to
     clear up uncertainties, mysteries, and doubts. In the
     early novels, he limited his irritability to human folly.
     In The Anti-Death League, he takes on God and the problem
     of good and evil, also. Notes an increase in hostility
     since Lucky Jim. The jokers become more ruthless with God
     as the ultimate sub-human joker in The Anti-Death League.
     Concludes that this is an unsatisfying but moving novel,
     "too timid to engage the problems it raises."

17   COOK, RODERICK. "Books in Brief." Harper's Magazine, 232
     (March), 152.
        Brief review of The Egyptologists. A very funny book
     which could make a good movie.

18   DAVENPORT, GUY. "A Round of the Same." National Review, 18
     (22 March), 279.

1966

Review of <u>The Egyptologist</u>. This is a weak farce for the humor is not sustained. The reader reads on only because he is curious to find out who or what the Egyptologists are.

19 _____. "Two Flops and a Winner." <u>National Review</u>, 18 (6 September), 893-894.
Review of <u>The Anti-Death League</u>. Calls this a "spoof on English manners." The fun develops as Amis lets his characters' disguises slip. From the fun, Amis emerges "as one of the best-natured comic writers in the business." He has mellowed in this novel; his temperament is now one of forgiveness.

20 DETWEILER, ROBERT. "God as the Enemy." <u>Christian Century</u>, 83 (12 October), 1242.
Review of <u>The Anti-Death League</u>. Amis is at the top of his form with this compelling novel, the best since <u>Lucky Jim</u>. Instead of a single anti-hero, there are many, all fighting against imminent death. To his credit, Amis uses the spy thriller narrative rather than a stock theological setting to advocate "love as a redeemer."

21 ELLIOTT, GEORGE P. "Nihilism for the Camera's Eye." <u>The New York Times</u> (21 August), part 7, p. 4.
Review of <u>The Anti-Death League</u>. Says this reads like a movie script. The funny scenes could have been funnier if they had been filmed or developed further. The plot is improbable, acceptable only if it goes by quickly, as in a film. Amis is saying something, but "the nihilism of the characters' world has infiltrated the author's handling of it."

22 EVANS, ROBERT O. "A Perspective for American Novelists." <u>Topic: A Journal of the Liberal Arts</u>, 12 (June), 64-66.
Review of <u>The Anti-Death League</u>. Amis deals with themes that are important in present society. His examination of man's place in a highly organized, mechanized society of nuclear weapons is essentially ethical.

23 FREMONT-SMITH, ELIOT. "Two Talented Authors, Two Disappointing Novels." <u>The New York Times</u> (12 August), p. 29L.
Review of <u>The Anti-Death League</u>. Amis controls his characters rigidly for the sake of a philosophical position; consequently, the characters are stifled, the plot is merely an "intricate harassment," and the philosophical position loses dramatic interest and relevancy. "Man's problem is to survive in the face of nasty God, or of a God in a nasty mood."

24 FRIEDLANDER, JANET. "New Books Appraised: Fiction." <u>Library</u>
    <u>Journal</u>, 91 (1 February), 711.
        Review of <u>The Egyptologists.</u> An amoral tale in which
    Amis underplays the humor and overplays the mystery. The
    plot and characters are slight. It might have been better
    as a short story.

25 GOLDMAN, ALBERT. "Calculated cackles." <u>The New York Herald</u>
    <u>Tribune Book Week</u> (10 April), p. 9.
        Review of <u>The Egyptologists.</u> This novel falls into the
    tradition of De Quincey's <u>Murder Considered as One of the</u>
    <u>Fine Arts,</u> but it fails in effect because the authors "do
    not establish a sharp and consistent counterpoint between
    propriety and indecency."

26 GRAVER, LAWRENCE. "The Curious Theology of Kingsley Amis."
    <u>The New Republic</u>, 155 (13 August), 26-28.
        Review of <u>The Anti-Death League.</u> This is a new departure
    for Amis, especially because his characters take on a new
    dignity from their efforts to deal with a malicious, unfa-
    miliar God and because Amis skillfully establishes a threat-
    ening atmosphere. There are, however, a number of weaknesses
    in the novel. As a comedy, for example, the novel offers
    little. As a moral statement, the problem is that the power
    the characters are fighting is metaphysical rather than
    social, and Amis is less confident about its origins. Con-
    sequently, the protest becomes repetitious and never deepens.
    This, together with excessive sympathy for the characters
    and a heavy reliance on plot and determinism, flattens the
    characters. Concludes by saying that as entertainment, the
    book succeeds, but as "a book about complex people suffering
    under God's dark design, it is more vulnerable. The gain
    is in range and daring; the loss in surefootedness."

27 GRAY, SIMON. "How Well Have they Worn? 5. <u>Lucky Jim</u>."
    London <u>Times</u> (3 February), p. 15.
        Assesses the <u>Lucky Jim</u> phenomenon, asserting it is still
    a simple book. "Its world is divided into fools and their
    pretensions, honest men and their appetites." The honest
    men "share a decent reticence about their real selves."
    The novel shares affinities with Whitehall and Wodehouse.
    Amis made use of society around him, and especially of one
    of its most sacred institutions. It was greeted as revolu-
    tionary because he was up-to-date. The hostile reactions
    amounted to "reflex rank-closing."

28 GRIFFINS, JOHN. "SF." London <u>Sunday Times</u> (10 April), p. 44.
    Brief mention of <u>Spectrum I.</u>

1966

29 HATCH, ROBERT. "A Tour of the Pops." Nation, 203 (5 December),
    620-621.
        Brief mention of The Anti-Death League. A "sardonic
    novel" whose tone of mockery is well sustained.

30 HILL, S.J., WILLIAM B. "Fiction." America, 115 (26 November),
    708.
        Brief mention of The Anti-Death League. A conventional
    spy novel but with the sophisticated satire and profundity
    expected of Amis.

31 HOPKINS, ROBERT H. "The Satire of Kingsley Amis's I Like It
    Here." Critique, 8 (Spring-Summer), 62-70.
        Calls I Like It Here a first-rate satire on Leavis' view
    of fiction and the "Angry Young Man" myths and a self-par-
    ody of clichés of the earlier novels. This is also an
    "aesthetic satire," a novel of literary attack. In the end,
    Amis makes a case for Fielding's fiction and, thus, for his
    own.

32 JENNINGS, ELIZABETH. "Farewell Blues." The Spectator, 216
    (18 March), 334.
        Review of The Anti-Death League. This novel is somewhat
    reminiscent of Orwell's 1984. Although it has all the in-
    gredients of a spy thriller, Amis is essentially concerned
    with people. Though not a stylistic advance, this is an
    advance in Amis' feelings for, and understanding of, human
    beings. Sees a resemblance between Catharine and Jenny
    Bunn.

33 KITCHING, JESSIE. "Forecasts." Publishers' Weekly, 189 (17
    January), 130-131.
        Brief review of The Egyptologists. There is little ac-
    tion, and the characterization and dialogue are obscure for
    most of the novel.

34 KREUTZ, IRVING. "Mrs. Trollope, Move Over!" Arts in Society,
    3 (Summer), 604-608.
        Notes a similarity between One Fat Englishman and Dickens'
    Martin Chuzzlewit. Both are satirical novels using an
    American college or university as a backdrop. Both feature
    heroes who, after a stay in the United States, can hardly
    wait to get home to England. Also sees similarities between
    Amis' novel and Wilfrid Sheed's A Middle Class Education,
    Pamela Hansford Johnson's Night and Silence Who Is Here?
    and Malcolm Bradbury's Stepping Westward. All feature an
    anti-hero whose grossness is monumental. Calls Micheldene
    "a kind of black-comedy Mr. Pickwick." Unlike Bradbury's

and Sheed's novels, Roger is not a new innocent abroad. Unlike all of the novelists, Amis stays with one point of
view, Roger's, and through it he satirizes America; and yet,
because it's told with Roger's words, we grin. Concludes
by showing that only Amis gives American undergraduates the
potential for being "funny, intelligent, and pleasant at
times."

35 LASKI, MARGHANITA. "Science Fiction." The Observer (13 Feb-
    ruary), p. 26.
        Brief recommendation of Spectrum III.

36 LEIBER, FRITZ. "Books." Magazine of Fantasy and Science Fic-
    tion, 30 (June), 39-40.
        Brief remarks on Spectrum IV, including summary of
    contents.

37 LEWIS, R.W. "Son of Lucky Jim Meets 007." Life, 61 (19 Au-
    gust), 8.
        Review of The Anti-Death League. Calls this a major ef-
    fort, a most ambitious novel, "an affort to extend the
    traditional comedy of manners...to take account of a great
    range of the spiritual dilemmas and dizzying absurdities
    that define contemporary life." Amis comes close to achiev-
    ing "a truly comic vision of the truly appalling."

38 LINDROTH, J.R. "Book Reviews." America, 115 (17 September),
    295-296.
        Review of The Anti-Death League. Because of the heavy
    symbolic weight given to characters, this is a unique spy
    thriller in which Amis probes man's capacity for love and
    dignity. The book is constructed around a series of ironies,
    and its meaning derived from Amis' compassion for human
    beings and his faith in them.

39 LODGE, DAVID. "Defying the Lightning." Tablet, 220 (26 March),
    360.
        Review of The Anti-Death League. "Since Lucky Jim, Amis'
    comedy has been increasingly permeated by undertones of fear
    and despair and disgust." In his latest novel, the comedy
    is incidental and slight. The novel is a logical develop-
    ment from Amis' short stories and interest in science fic-
    tion. Like Greene's entertainments, The Anti-Death League
    seems to be aiming at the effect "where the conventions of
    popular fiction are turned to a serious moral and philosoph-
    ical purpose." Remarks there are some incongruities about
    the British government challenging God.

1966

40 _____. "The Modern, the Contemporary, and the Importance of
   Being Amis," in his Language of Fiction: Essays in Crit-
   ical and Verbal Analysis of the English Novel. London:
   Routledge and Kegan Paul; New York: Columbia University
   Press, pp. 243-267.
        Reprint of 1963.B19.

41 McCABE, BERNARD. "The ADL." Commonweal, 85 (25 November),
   237.
        Review of The Anti-Death League. The novel is marked by
   anger and violence, but developed through comedy. As in
   Lucky Jim, Amis quickly identifies the enemies and confronts
   anger head-on. In this case, death is the issue. "The novel is a deliberate cathartic exercise," but the ending is
   unresolved.

42 McNAMARA, EUGENE. "The Egyptologists." America, 114 (30
   April), 630-631.
        Review of The Egyptologists. This is an "elaborate
   parody," but also a long, unfunny, boring work without any
   humorous possibilities whatsoever.

43 MADDOCKS, MELVIN. "New Novels in Review." Christian Science
   Monitor (18 August), p. 5.
        Review of The Anti-Death League. Amis creates an ominous
   "world-within-a-world" in which he finds horrible the bland-
   ness of the officers in face of horror. This is a philosophical confrontation with the problem of evil, but the
   debate is beyond Amis and "only tends to turn him hysterical
   and profane." Notes that as Amis likes life less, he ap-
   pears to like people more.

44 MALOFF, SAUL. "Books." Commonweal, 84 (6 May), 203-204.
        Review of The Egyptologists. This is Amis' "worst and
   most trivial book." The mystery is tiresome, and the reader
   is duped into expecting more than he is given by the end.

45 MATTHEWS, T.S. "High Jinks in a Back Street." The New York
   Times Book Review (6 February), p. 4.
        Review of The Egyptologists. This novel would be better
   as a movie. Because there's nothing really funny about
   sex, the "elaborate little jokes leave an unpleasant taste."

46 MEHOKE, JAMES S. "Sartre's Theory of Emotion and Three English
   Novelists: Waugh, Greene, and Amis." Wisconsin Studies in
   Literature, 3 (Spring), 105-113.
        Finds in the novels of Waugh, Greene and Amis a return
   to the 18th century picaro as a confidence man, an Everyman

figure in a Confidence World. These confidence men become useful instruments of society and fall into two general types: (1) Those who succeed in maintaining their deceptive roles and (2) those who are detected because they find their roleplaying so painful. The latter become victims of their own deceit.

47 MOON, ERIC. "Fiction." Library Journal, 91 (July), 3464.
    Review of The Anti-Death League. This is Amis' most ambitious and most complicated novel to date. It has two major themes: (1) the "inevitability and cruel illogic of death" and (2) the "exploration of the topical 'god is dead' debate."

48 MORSE, J. MITCHELL. "Fiction Chronicle." Hudson Review, 19 (Autumn), 511.
    Brief review of The Anti-Death League. Amis is a "trashy writer" and a "harmless rebel." Excerpted: 1973.B33.

49 NIGHTINGALE, BENEDICT. "Science Fiction." The Observer (30 October), p. 28.
    Brief review of Spectrum V. Except for James H. Schmitz's story, the collection is a "dull, conventional grind."

50 PRYCE-JONES, ALAN. "A Bit Funny in a Terribly British Way." The New York Herald Tribune (22 February), p. 15.
    Review of The Egyptologists. The novel is "entirely local in tone" and may appeal to the British sense of humor. However, the "whole effect of the book is spoiled by its absence of high spirits." No amount of comic detail "can compensate for the testiness of mind which lies behind every joke."

51 RABINOVITZ, RUBIN. "Reaction Against Experimentalism in the English Novel: 1950-60." Ph.D. dissertation, Columbia University.
    See 1967.B28 and 1976.B20 for annotation and excerpt.

52 RAVEN, SIMON. "Skeleton at the feast." The Observer (20 March), p. 27.
    In the early novels there is, beneath the laughter, "hints of the sadness, the unkindness, the frailty of things." In Take A Girl Like You, this element of melancholy becomes overt and prominent, for the origins of laughter are often gloomy and its efficacy often dubious. One Fat Englishman is dominated by a pessimistic tone and "a tough, pagan disposition to take the best as it came and expect the worse." The Anti-Death League, however, is

1966

disappointing because Amis has become "querulous and shrill."
Because of a lack of control, the theme isn't controlled
and developed. As a suspense story, it is excellent, but
a story without morality is a story out-of-balance.

53   RICKS, CHRISTOPHER. "Operation Malvolio." New Statesman, 71
         (18 March), 387.
            Review of The Anti-Death League. Although Amis' concern
      with death is real, and although we share Churchill's fears
      and superstitions, the novel is hard to take seriously be-
      cause of Caton's appearance. He is a figure from another
      world, and the world surrounding Catharine, Dr. Best, and
      Churchill collapses when Caton enters. Also, this novel
      shares properties with The Egyptologists, and this may be
      a part of the problem. If it were not for the malevolent
      Dr. Best, it would be easy to despise Ayscue, Leonard, Lady
      Hazell, and Hunter. Amis seems to have it in for Dr. Best
      who, as Malvolio, is "graced with the most telling comic
      effects."

54   NO ENTRY.

55   ROSENTHAL, RAYMOND. "The Nub of the Node." New Leader, 49
         (1 August), 18-19.
            Review of The Anti-Death League. This is a new genre--
      half high comedy and half farce--and yet neither is devel-
      oped with enough force to come off. Amis is not decisive
      about the problem he touches on. The novel doesn't have
      the easygoing morality we saw in the earlier novels. More-
      over, the "metaphysical thrusts" are blunted by the happy
      endings.

56   ROTONDARO, FRED. "Fiction." Best Sellers, 26 (15 April),
         26-27.
            Brief mention of The Egyptologists.

57   RYAN, S.P. "Fiction." Best Sellers, 26 (15 August), 178.
            Review of The Anti-Death League. In this novel much of
      Amis' comic flair has returned to be combined with an atmo-
      sphere of doom. That he has recaptured his comic touch is
      most important of all. Much of this is a thesis about his
      anti-death, anti-war philosophy. The final message is ob-
      scure, however.

58 SHUTTLEWORTH, MARTIN. "An Effort at Yea-saying." Punch, 250
      (30 March), 473.
            Review of The Anti-Death League. Amis discusses God and
      the problem of evil, but as a whole the book is a failure,
      "a failure in a direction and on a scale enormously worth
      failing at." Sees parallels with Flaubert (as satirist)
      and Fleming (as spy thriller).

59 STURGEON, THEODORE. "Fine Fat Packages." The National Review,
      18 (25 January), 78.
            Brief mention of Spectrum IV.

60 TEMPLE, RUTH Z. and MARTIN TUCKER, comps. "Kingsley Amis," in
      A Library of Literary Criticism: Modern British Literature.
      Vol. VI: New York: Ungar, pp. 10-13.
            Excerpted: 1955.B16; 1958.B19; 1960.B9, B18; 1964.B2-B4.

61 VOORHEES, RICHARD J. "Wodehouse and English Literature," in
      his P.G. Wodehouse. Twayne English Authors Series, edited
      by Sylvia E. Bowman. Boston: Twayne Publishers, p. 182.
            Says Amis owes much to Wodehouse's technique of farce.

62 WALSH, JOHN. "In a Protest Against Unreason, Jolly Mr. Amis
      Turns Tragedian." The Observer (26 September), p. 23.
            Review of The Anti-Death League. Amis' theme is somber.
      "It is the old question of death without judgment, of men's
      fates being often decided with little regard to what they
      do or deserve." Most of the characters are fallible; there
      are no superhuman heroes or archvillains. Moreover, Amis
      presents no new insights, but "a protest against inhumanity
      and unreason, a protest with neither solution nor
      consolation."

63 _____. "There's Hanky-Panky, But Laughs Are Limited in Two
      British Books." The National Observer (14 February), p. 23.
            Review of The Egyptologists. The concept is amusing,
      but it becomes labored at this length. Wonders why Amis,
      a successful novelist, would team up with Robert Conquest
      to produce such "foolishness." Although the dialogue is
      brisk and witty and reminiscent of Wodehouse, "from time to
      time a kind of reality breaks in, which Wodehouse never per-
      mits, and as a result the Egyptologists' antics are more
      furtive than funny."

64 WEST, PAUL. "The Destructive Element." The New York Herald
      Tribune Book Week. (14 August), pp. 1, 12.
            Review of The Anti-Death League. In his first four nov-
      els, Amis dealt with opponents of love, "cant, snobbery,

1966

labels, abstractions, status, and so on," seeking to prove
that nothing endures except integrity. In his latest novel,
for the first time, we see Amis "as a writer of tenderness,
compassion, or sense of mystery." Also sees Amis as "a
writer capable of overlapping William Golding and Graham
Greene through an interest in things spiritual or, in the
widest sense, religious." In this novel, Amis "begins to
write undeludedly and unshallowly about love as well as pain
and death." This marks a breakthrough for Amis, from entertainer to "a scrutineer of humanity."

65 WORDSWORTH, CHRISTOPHER. "Amis In Deep." Manchester Guardian
      (18 March), p. 7.
          Review of The Anti-Death League. "In our beginnings are
      our ends, and although Mr. Amis has not succeeded in graft-
      ing his parable he remains sharply entertaining, while sug-
      gesting that he is no longer content to be merely that."
      Reprinted: 1966.B66.

66 _____. "Amis in deeper waters." Manchester Guardian Weekly,
      94 (24 March), 11.
          Reprint of 1966.B65.

67 YOUNG, B.A. "Space-Time." Punch, 251 (9 November), 719.
          Brief mention of Spectrum V, in which he disagrees with
      the introduction.

1967 A BOOKS - NONE

1967 B SHORTER WRITINGS

1   ANON. "Announcements." Kirkus, 35 (15 January), 86.
          Brief mention of Spectrum V, noting that the stories
      end on an optimistic note.

2   ANON. "Lucky Jim Bond." Newsweek, 68 (8 May), 61.
          Interview with Amis on Colonel Sun. Amis says he envis-
      ages "a slightly more cerebral Bond, solving mysteries with
      mind over mayhem and casting witty asides on the social
      scene." He admits he won't capture the "aristocratic savoir-
      faire" Fleming was noted for.

3   ANON. "Notes on Current Books." Virginia Quarterly Review,
      43 (Winter), xiv.
          Review of The Anti-Death League. A sharp departure for
      Amis. All is dead serious, for Amis has turned into a sober
      moralist. The message has precedence over the art, so most

of the wisdom and fun abundant in earlier novels is missing
in this one.

4   ANON. "What About You? What About Me?" The Times Literary
     Supplement (23 November), p. 1106.
          Review of A Look Round the Estate. Behind the erotic
     emerges the hand of death in these poems. Notes a resem-
     blance between Amis and the character Evans; this is a key
     to the "vulnerable tone" of the poetry. This vulnerability
     "depends on our teetering disbelief in Evan's apparent op-
     portunism, crude sensuality and mistrust of art or love."

5   BRIEN, ALAN. "Amis goes pop." New Statesman, 74 (7 July),
     15-16.
          Discusses Amis' public attitude. "He has always been an
     expert at showing us how we deceive ourselves in the very
     act of congratulating ourselves on not being deceived....The
     essence of his public attitude has been summed up in 'You
     can't take me in.' His motto was--'No Bullshit.'" Ex-
     cerpted: 1973.B33.

6   BROICH, ULRICH. "Tradition und Rebellion." Poetica, 1 (April),
     220-221.
          Discusses Lucky Jim as a picaresque novel. (In German.)

7   BUFKIN, E.C. "Kingsley Amis," in The Twentieth-Century Novel
     in English: A Checklist. Athens: University of Georgia
     Press, p. 3.
          Lists Amis' novels through 1966, together with information
     on his publishers in England.

8   BURGESS, ANTHONY. "A Sort of Rebels," in his The Novel Now:
     A Guide to Contemporary Fiction. New York: Norton, pp.
     141-144.
          Finds a post-war restiveness in Lucky Jim, and calls
     Amis the "voice of decent protest" whose dominant theme is
     "hypergamy." Dixon is the most popular anti-hero of our
     time; he is against culture "because culture has the wrong
     associations." Mentions all of the novels through One Fat
     Englishman, and concludes that Amis belongs to the tradition
     of English nonconformism in Defoe and Fielding. Excerpted:
     1973.B47.

9   BUSH, ALFRED L. "Literary Landmarks of Princeton." Princeton
     University Library Chronicle, 29 (Autumn), 75-76.
          Memoir of Amis' year at Princeton (1958). While there,
     he wrote New Maps of Hell and part of Take A Girl Like You,
     along with four poems. As for One Fat Englishman, he says

1967

the house and neighborhood at Princeton "gave me material for some of the physical ambience" of the novel.

10 CASSON, ALLAN. "Greene's Comedians And Amis's Anti-Death League." Massachusetts Review, 8 (Spring), 395-397.
The Anti-Death League is coherent only as an entertainment in the Graham Greene sense, and so it might be better as a movie. It is a comedy thriller with a romantic lead who is both officer and manipulator of most of the action. It is also a combination love story and tragic farce of a spy plot. The funny clash between Best and Leonard recalls Lucky Jim. Regarding the religious issues in the novel, to take the first three-quarters seriously leaves the ending incongruous. Concludes that there is material here for two good novels. As it stands, it is incoherent.

11 COCKBURN, ALEXANDER. "Striking Poses." New Statesman, 73 (24 March), 414.
Political attack on Amis in which Cockburn wonders how Amis ever came to the position he has of attacking the Communist influence among liberals.

12 CONQUEST, ROBERT. "Counsels for Defense." The Times Literary Supplement (18 May), p. 419.
Recounts a wager he made with Amis concerning the overuse of the word "infanticide" in the press.

13 COOPER, R.W. "The Amis View of Bond." London Times (26 April), p. 8.
Report on Amis' appearance on BBC 1's Twenty-Four Hours Programme. Amis defends himself against the charge that he might be a weak imitator of Fleming by saying that while some changes in Bond's tastes are inferred in Colonel Sun, the thriller allows room for asides on the social scene.

14 DICK, BERNARD F. "Epilogue," in his William Golding. Twayne English Authors Series, edited by Sylvia E. Bowman. Boston: Twayne Publishers, p. 102.
Amis, in an attempt to categorize Golding, suggests that Golding is only a serious writer working within a framework of science fiction. His opinions are not, however, conclusive.

15 FLEISCHMANN, WOLFGANG BERNARD, comp. "Kingsley Amis," in Encyclopedia of World Literature in the Twentieth Century. Vol. I. New York: Ungar, p. 44.
Brief biographical comments together with a bibliography, both primary and secondary. In One Fat Englishman, he says,

we see new dimensions to Amis' satiric skill. My Enemy's
Enemy "demonstrates Amis' growing realization that the
coarse make-up of his earlier heroes can, in itself, be the
object of satire."

16   FULLER, ROY. "Estate Duties." The Listener, 78 (9 November),
        609-610.
            Review of A Look Round the Estate. Notes an "earthiness"
        to Amis' poetry and a pure moral sense. The earlier poems
        lapse into "simplicity" and "feebleness," whereas the later
        poems are much better. The language is natural, the narra-
        tion is skillful, and the details are right. Finds in Amis'
        poetry "the ethical acuteness and insight into behavior"
        that brought him fame.

17   GARDNER, AURORA WEST. "Fiction." Library Journal, 92 (15
        March), 1175.
            Unfavorable mention of Spectrum V. Finds it hard to
        justify the stories in the collection.

18   GRIGG, JOHN. "Mr. Amis abdicates." Manchester Guardian (6
        July), p. 16.
            Looks for similarities between Amis' experiences and
        those of a new generation of writers.

19   HAMILTON, IAN. "Dead ends and soft centres." The Observer
        (12 November), p. 28.
            Review of A Look Round the Estate. Sees no signs of real
        development in Amis as a poet since A Case of Samples. Amis
        continues to be "amusing, skillful, posturing, soft-cen-
        tered." He keeps trying to write poetry, and although he
        starts serious, we know a joke is at the end. Excerpted:
        1973.B33.

20   HOLMES, RICHARD. "Poets: Ferlinghetti, Amis, Coward, and
        Love, love, love." London Times (16 December), p. 18.
            Review of A Look Round the Estate. Amis' poems epito-
        mize what was "best, sharp and flippant in 50's English
        verse." Amis wars against middle class respectabilities
        and often ends with a note of disappointment.

21   KAVANAGH, P.J. "Amis country." Manchester Guardian Weekly,
        97 (16 November), 11.
            Reprint of 1967.B21.

22   _____. "The Evans Country." Manchester Guardian (10 November),
        p. 7.
            Review of A Look Round the Estate. Since Lucky Jim,

1967

there has been at the center of all of Amis' novels a protagonist who refuses to refer back to what he should be
feeling and who relishes cheerfully what he does feel. This
note is sounded in his poems. Amis is entertaining because
he is unpredictable.

23   KITCHING, JESSIE. "Forecasts." Publishers' Weekly, 191 (9
        January), p. 59.
             Brief mention of Spectrum V. The story-telling is good
        and the gimmicks are convincing.

24   LEWIS, ANTHONY. "Amis Is Writing James Bond Book." The New
        York Times (25 April), p. 38.
             Report of an interview with Amis, who says he is trying
        to write in the style of Fleming. Finds this harder work
        than his own. Whether or not he writes more Bond novels
        depends on how this first one is received.

25   OAKES, PHILIP. "Rising Sun." London Sunday Times (22 October),
        p. 11.
             Review of Colonel Sun. The props are standard Fleming,
        and the plot is as ritualistic as any Fleming could hope
        for.

26   ORESTOV, OLEY. "Koponka Kommentatora: London Adyenskye
        Vodorovot." Pravda (23 June), p. 5.
             Personal attack on Amis and his writings. (In Russian.)

27   "POOTER." "Diary & gossip." London Times (14 October), p. 21.
             Report saying that because of too much pressure from
        other commitments, Amis and Conquest will probably discon-
        tinue the Spectrum series.

28   RABINOVITZ, RUBIN. Reaction Against Experimentalism in the
        English Novel: 1950-60. New York: Columbia University
        Press, pp. 38-63, 174-178.
             Examines Amis' literary judgments in his fiction, poetry,
        reviews, and nonfiction, and finds that Amis dislikes ex-
        perimentalism for its own sake. He prefers a more direct,
        conventional style, appealing to common sense and thus is
        similar to both 18th century and early 19th century nov-
        elists. His style is simple and straightforward; his plots
        are uncomplicated and chronological; his concerns are moral
        and social problems. "As for terms like 'Angry Young Man,'
        or 'liberal,' in Amis' case they obscure the issue more
        than anything else." Includes a detailed bibliography of
        primary and secondary materials to 1962. Expanded reprint
        of 1966.B51. Excerpted: 1976.B20.

29 ROSENTHAL, M.L. The New Poets: American and British Poetry
     Since World War II. New York: Oxford University Press,
     pp. 199, 200, 236, 320.
          Comments on Amis' poetry as it relates to The Movement
     and as it has affected British poetry.

30 SYMONS, JULIAN. "Down with Romance." New Statesman, 74 (1
     December), 780.
          Review of A Look Round the Estate. "These poems, always
     neat and dexterous, sometimes funny, belong in style to the
     'down with Romance, even poets fart' manner of the early
     'Fifties, when colloquial language was a useful corrective
     to Dylanesque rhetoric." But this is not true now. "The
     most successful poems here attempt least."

31 WELCH, COLIN. "Waiting for Lefty." The Spectator, 219 (21
     July), 75.
          Expresses resentment for Amis' shift to a Tory point of
     view. To be a Conservative requires no brains at all, for
     one must just accept what exists.

1968 A BOOKS - NONE

1968 B SHORTER WRITINGS

1 ADAMS, PHOEBE. "Short Reviews." Atlantic Monthly, 221 (June),
     124.
          Brief unfavorable mention of Colonel Sun.

2 ADLER, DICK. "Portrait of A Man Reading." Book World, 2 (20
     October), 8.
          Interview with Amis covering his reading habits, prepa-
     tions for writing Colonel Sun, science fiction anthologies,
     and interest in G.K. Chesterton and Sherlock Holmes.

3 AMORY, CLEVELAND. "Cosmo Reads the New Books." Cosmopolitan,
     165 (July), 12.
          Review of Colonel Sun. Bond has grown "an inconvenient
     conscience." Calls this the best and most believable novel
     to date in the Bond series.

4 ANON. "Impersonations." The Listener, 79 (11 January), 48.
          Memoir of Amis reading his verse aloud and his enjoyment
     of parody.

5 ANON. "Unlucky James." The Times Literary Supplement (28
     March), p. 309.

1968

> Review of <u>Colonel Sun</u>. Calls Amis' Bond "a chuckle-
> headed imposter." The few amusing moments are accidental,
> and nothing in the novel rings true because unlike Amis,
> Fleming believed in what he wrote.

6   ANON. "Amis is Thrilled About Thrillers." <u>The New York Times</u>
>   (25 April), p. 44.
>   Notes that <u>Colonel Sun</u> is well received by the public and
> attacked by the critics. Amis reacts to this by saying he
> enjoyed the travels taken to Mexico to write the book. Says
> he has enjoyed thrillers ever since he was young.

7   ANON. "The Thinking Man's 007." <u>Time</u>, 91 (10 May), 125.
>   Review of <u>Colonel Sun</u>. This is "a reasonably healthy,
> if slightly pale, replica," but it lacks much of the "comic-
> book charm" of Fleming. Amis discards technical gimmickry,
> and this, together with an unfortunately obvious develop-
> ment, weakens the novel.

8   ANON. "Coming Obituaries: 5: Kingsley Amis: Ex-wit and
>   ghost." <u>Punch</u>, 225 (28 August), 297.
>   Satirizes Amis' political switch and his Bond novel.

9   ANON. "In A Buyer's Market." <u>The Times Literary Supplement</u>
>   (10 October), p. 1145.
>   Review of <u>I Want It Now</u>. This is a "banal study" of
> character development. Although the "comedy of discomfort"
> is good, the moralizing and satire undermine the story. It
> is hard to know who's making all the observations.

10   ANON. "Lost Leader." <u>The Listener</u>, 80 (7 November), 610.
>   Amis comments that after his political switch, he noted
> some change in the critics' attitude but none by the general
> reader. Says the public wants a readable book that is hu-
> morous from time to time.

11   BAKER, ROGER. "No touch." London <u>Times</u> (30 March), p. 21.
>   Review of <u>Colonel Sun</u>. This is a "pale copy" of Fleming.
> Missing is the sophisticated hedonism that made a popular
> hero of Bond. Moreover, the heroes and villains lack
> Fleming's "off-beat kinkiness." The description is clichéd
> and there's a lack of mechanical aids to help Bond in fights.

12   BLACKBURN, TOM. "The Poet as Craftsman." <u>Poetry Review</u>, 59
>   (Spring), 57.
>   Review of <u>A Look Round the Estate</u>. Many of these poems
> "show the contemporary desire not to be taken in by any
> ideal or experience." The best poems are both "wittily

serious and skillfully off-hand." Says "Nothing to Fear" concerns the "illusion of being able to take adultery lightly and without guilt." "The Evans Country" expresses "a Chaucerian relish of the human comedy whose characters so rarely understand the vast gap between what they preach and what they practise." Excerpted: 1973.B33.

13 BOYLE, T.E., and BROWN, T. "The Serious Side of Kingsley Amis's Lucky Jim." Critique: Studies in Modern Fiction, 9 (Spring), 100-107.
Discusses Lucky Jim as more than a comic novel; beneath the comedy Amis offers some pessimistic comments on the human condition. Like Huckleberry Finn and The Catcher in the Rye, the novel reflects what existentialists call "the absurd," which Dixon faces up to. The humor results from the disparity between the protagonist's expectations and harsh reality. In an attempt to cope with reality, Dixon retreats behind faces and games. Blind luck rules the world. The effects of dishonest self-denial are dehumanizing. Excerpted: 1973.B33.

14 BRADBURY, MALCOLM. "Bond dishonoured." Manchester Guardian (29 March), p. 12.
Review of Colonel Sun. Lacks a convincing rhetoric, The Fleming specialties are "muted," and the novel is marred by a weak plot and stock villains. "The famous exotic world of Fleming gets cut down uncomfortably to size by the equally famous world of the Amis reality principle." Reprint: 1968.B16.

15 _____. "Delayed Orgasm." New Statesman, 76 (11 October), 464, 466.
Calls Amis a kind of contemporary Jane Austen because of his resolution to I Want It Now. Says Amis' moralism is obvious in the outcome. Notes that as Amis' heroes develop, they become not only detectors of bastards, but bastards themselves. Says there's not much that is culturally exact in the novel. It is "a bit too much a 1960's novelist triumphing over 1920's characters." Amis gives hints of broadening his range, trying to leave the confines of the sociomoral novel.

16 _____. "not so lucky Bond." Manchester Guardian Weekly, 98 (18 April), 10.
Reprint of 1968.B14.

17 BRODIE, IAN. "Why I Took on 007--by Kingsley Amis." London Daily Express (16 March), p. 8.

1968

        Interview in which Amis comments on his writing of
Colonel Sun.

18   BUCKLEY, P.L. "Books in Brief." National Review, 20 (18 June),
       619.
           Review of Colonel Sun. If the novel were not about Bond,
this would be a great spy story. As a Bond thriller, however, it is disappointing to Fleming fans. Although it is
a mirror image of Bond, it is not authentic because Bond
remains true to one woman, has moral scruples, is decent,
and is too close to the ideological line toward Communism.

19   BURGESS, ANTHONY. "Amis and Enemies." The Listener, 80 (10
       October), 475.
           Notes "something approaching an emergent moral philos-
ophy" in Amis. I Want It Now is especially meaningful when
compared to Lucky Jim, for now we see that Dixon was striving
for the good life and to change things. Ronnie succeeds in
changing himself, and the book is ultimately about being
better. In its moral protest against the rich, the book is
funny, serious and wonderfully readable.

20   COLE, BARRY. "Vintage Stuff." The Spectator, 221 (11 October),
       516.
           Review of I Want It Now. The hero is in search of "great
expectations," but the novel "does little more than up-date
and extend the conclusions" of Lucky Jim.

21   CONROY, MARY. "A hero in his place." London Times (12 Oc-
       tober), p. 24.
           Review of I Want It Now. The best part of the novel is
Ronnie's character, for he has the "traditional Amis qualities of wit, singlemindedness, and ambition." Unlike the
traditional Amis hero, however, Ronnie is in a world to
which these qualities are appropriate. He is the first of
the Amis heroes to make it on his own. Also comments on
sexual success (which has been sharpened), girls (as inse-
cure as the men), satire on the rich (overdone) and on the
television world (more satisfying).

22   CRISPIN, EDMUND. "Bond reborn." London Sunday Times (31
       March), p. 55.
           Review of Colonel Sun. Argues that Bond appears too
kindly for his own good in both Fleming and Amis. Also,
sex is quite puritan in both and the hero is ruthless, but
in "the animal, méchant sense."

23   CUFF, SERGEANT. "Criminal Record: Fiction." Saturday Review,
       51 (29 June), 30.
           Brief mention of Colonel Sun.

24   D., D.M. "Other New Books of Poetry." The National Observer
       (9 September), p. B4.
           Review of A Look Round the Estate. Amis is "unfailingly
       entertaining" in this collection. "After Goliath" is "a
       chilling attack on intellectual pretension."

25   ENRIGHT, D.J. "A Cloud that's Dragonish." The Listener, 79
       (28 March), 411.
           Review of Colonel Sun. In this novel a new Bond hero
       emerges with more acute scruples. The most interesting as-
       pect of the book is its morality, for Amis seems to be en-
       couraging the reader to hate and fear the East, but not
       much that is positive is said for the rest of the world
       either. "Bond appears to be offering a choice not so much
       between being dead and being Red as between two forms of
       deadness."

26   EWART, GAVIN. "Entertainers." The London Magazine, NS 7
       (January), 102-104.
           Review of A Look Round the Estate. An entertaining book,
       neither solemn nor pretentious.

27   GOFF, FRANCIS. "James Into Jim." London Sunday Telegraph
       (31 March), p. 11.
           Brief mention of Colonel Sun. Refers to Lucky Jim as he
       comments on Amis' innovative change from the academic novel
       to the James Bond thriller.

28   GRANT, VIOLET. "Criminal Records." London Daily Telegraph
       (28 March), p. 22.
           Brief favorable review of Colonel Sun with plot summary.

29   HAMILTON, IAN. "Recent Fiction." London Daily Telegraph
       (10 October), p. 23.
           Says I Want It Now is "a subtle oblique fable" with an
       ending that is thoroughly satisfactory.

30   HARRIS, LEO. "Lucky James." Punch, 254 (23 April), 619.
           Review of Colonel Sun. The novel is not convincing be-
       cause we don't feel that Amis, unlike Fleming, really meant
       what he wrote. Bond is less dominant and the climax less
       catastrophic than in a Fleming novel.

1968

31 HEPPENSTALL, RAYNER. "Bond rebound." The Spectator, 220
(29 March), 409-410.
Review of Colonel Sun. This is an enjoyable thriller
that some fans of Bond may find impalpable. Notes that
masochism doesn't come easily to Amis. The Greek island is
hardly exotic. Does see some "academicism" in language,
and says Amis' progressive past shows through.

32 HOPE, FRANCIS. "Appleyard among the millionaires." The Observer (6 October), p. 33.
Review of I Want It Now. This novel is "as sharp, as
unsparing, as agilely destructive as One Fat Englishman."
Unfortunately, Amis has to revert to a higher moral plane,
much like John Lewis in That Uncertain Feeling and Patrick
Standish in Take A Girl Like You. Ronnie redeems his rude-
ness by goodness much too quickly, as Amis "moves from cool
observation to sentimental slapstick, from a comedy of situation to a morality of stereotypes."

33 HORROCKS, NORMAN. "Fiction." Library Journal, 93 (1 April),
1500-1501.
Review of Colonel Sun. Says the gadgetry is less intru-
sive and the writing is tauter than in the earlier Bond
stories.

34 HUBIN, ALLEN. "Criminals At Large." The New York Times Book
Review (19 May), p. 32.
Review of Colonel Sun. Calls this a better book than
the last few Fleming originals.

35 JENNINGS, ELIZABETH. "Poetry, Formal & Formless." London
Daily Telegraph (7 March), p. 21.
Brief review of A Look Round the Estate. Focuses on
Amis' technique.

36 KING, FRANCIS. "Stingy Rich." London Sunday Telegraph (6
October), p. 12.
Brief mention of I Want It Now with a summary of the
plot.

37 KNOWLES, A. SIDNEY, JR. "The Need for Loners: Nine Novels of
the Sixties." Southern Review, NS 4 (Summer) 820-823.
Review of The Anti-Death League. The novel is marred by
a chaotic and vague plot and by characters who become lost
or forgotten. It is "governed more by a kind of dilet-
tantish philosophizing than by the demands of art."

38   LEE, JAMES W. "Introduction," in his John Braine. Twayne
      English Authors Series, edited by Sylvia E. Bowman. Boston:
      Twayne Publishers, pp. 20-24.
          Jim Dixon, as a new post-war hero, expresses the disil-
      lusionment felt by many other characters. Irreverence to-
      wards the tradition of the British Establishment character-
      izes Dixon. Take A Girl Like You is the only novel to come
      to grips with the social problems of class, rural vs. urban
      values, and mass culture. Concludes that the influence of
      Lucky Jim is still being felt on the British novel and its
      writers.

39   LEJEUNE, ANTHONY. "Bond Renewed." Tablet, 222 (6 April),
      342-343.
          Review of Colonel Sun. Although this is "a very readable
      action-full thriller," one can't help being aware "that this
      is Kingsley Amis writing what he thinks Ian Fleming would
      have written." Missing is "a certain high gloss, a combi-
      nation of fantasy and worldliness, of a reporter's curios-
      ity with an Etonian confidence, of apparent ease with great
      professionalism." Concludes by saying that "Amis writes
      like a writer; Ian Fleming wrote like what he was--an up-
      perclass man of the world who happened in his youth to have
      been a foreign correspondent."

40   LEWIS, ANTHONY. "Yevtushenko Assailed in Britain As Soviet
      'Hack Propagandist.'" The New York Times (22 November),
      pp. 1, 16.
          Account of Amis' accusation that Yevtushenko denounced
      suppressed and imprisoned Soviet writers.

41   LISTER, RICHARD. "Here's bad news for Amis-haters--his new
      novel is a real corker." London Evening Standard (8 Oc-
      tober), p. 11.
          Brief favorable review of I Want It Now. Calls it one
      of Amis' best for its thematic content, characterization,
      and satire on the rich.

42   McDONALD, G.D. "Poetry." Library Journal, 93 (1 October),
      3566.
          Review of A Look Round the Estate. The collection is
      "rueful, candid, and ironical--concerned with people rather
      than things, and with sex placed high on the agenda."

43   McDOWELL, FRED P.W. "The Recent Novel in English." Contem-
      porary Literature, 9 (Autumn), 559, 562.
          Outlines Amis' literary theories as discussed by
      Rabinovitz. (See 1966.B51 and 1967.B28.)

1968

44   McGUINNESS, FRANK. Review of I Want It Now. The London Maga-
      zine, NS 8 (October), 110-114.
           Ronnie marks "a sad decline from those early brilliant
      days when his creator gave us the most engaging anti-hero
      since Tom Jones." This is an unreservedly bad book. Com-
      ments on Amis' politics and his appearance on television to
      promote the novel.

45   MAY, DERWENT. "Views." The Listener, 80 (26 December), 848.
           Review of I Want It Now. Amis pictures "ruthless greed
      and petty vanity" among the successful. This is a bitter
      novel, reflecting the moral inadequacy of the times.

46   MILLER, KARL. "Introduction," in his Writing in England Today:
      The Last Fifteen Years. Baltimore: Penguin Books, pp. 13-
      30, passim.
           Introductory material on the "Movement" and the "Angry
      Young Men."

*47   MORGAN, EDWIN. "In pursuit of Croesus." London Sunday Times
      (13 October), p. 63.
           Unlocatable. Listed incorrectly in 1976.A1.

48   MOYNAHAN, JULIAN. "A Look Round the Estate." The New York
      Times Book Review (22 December), p. 10.
           Brief mention of A Look Round the Estate. Calls it "ne-
      glectful and disappointing."

49   NICHOLS, LEWIS. "American Notebook: Bond-Markham-Amis." The
      New York Times Book Review (28 April), pp. 20-22.
           Memoir in which we are told Amis may write another Bond
      story because of his travels to Mexico.

50   NYE, ROBERT. "A rake's conversion." Manchester Guardian
      Weekly, 99 (17 October), 14.
           Reprint of 1968.B51.

51   _____. "A stink of sentimentality." Manchester Guardian (11
      October), p. 9.
           Review of I Want It Now. Ronnie's conversion would be
      convincing if Amis' early grip on the character had been
      sustained and if Ronnie had been shown to be still acting
      out of self-interest when he confronts Mrs. Baldock for the
      girl. So, Amis "sacrifices verisimilitude for a novelistic
      celebration of the power of virtue, with not enough empha-
      sis on the power."

52 OBERBECK, S.K. "The new James Bond: calmer music, weaker
    wine." Book World (5 May), part I, p. 5.
        Review of Colonel Sun. Notes a number of differences
    between Amis' Bond and Fleming's, including: (1) Amis'
    Bond is more vulnerable and more reliant on brains, muscles,
    guts, and guns; (2) Amis' Bond is "a sensitive man-of-ethics
    who suffers pangs of doubt and remorse over the 'senseless'
    violence of his profession"; (3) Amis' Bond is less the
    womanizer. "Though Amis uses the familiar Fleming script,
    his changes in Bond's character throw the formula askew.
    Consequently, Amis has transformed Bond into something he
    was never meant to be." He has humanized Bond. Excerpted:
    1973.B33.

53 PEREZ, GALLEGO, CANDIDO. Literatura y rebelida en la Ingla-
    terra actual: Los 'Angry Young Men,' una movimento social
    de los anos cincuenta. Madrid: Consejo Superior de In-
    vestigationes, 32 pp., passim.
        General survey of the "Angry Young Men" movement.

54 PRICE, R.G.G. "New Novels." Punch, 255 (16 October), 557.
        Review of I Want It Now. This is an entertaining novel
    in the Graham Greene sense. Amis is unique "in representing
    the latest, possibly the last, development of the noncon-
    formist conscience while accepting the world of bed and
    booze." Excerpted: 1973.B33.

55 _____. "Some Novels of '68." Punch, 255 (25 Decememeber), 931.
        Mention of I Want It Now as best novel of the year.
    This is one of Amis' best, despite the mixed reception by
    critics. Novel ends with the constant Amis theme, the
    emergence of goodness.

56 "R." "COLUMN." Encounter, 31 (September), 40-42.
        Studies the development of Amis, noting that in later
    novels he begins to worry as dark forces threaten life,
    liberty and the pursuit of happiness. Also comments on
    Amis' political stands, saying Amis' reasons for his polit-
    ical change seem hardly sufficient. Probably he changed
    because of his growing irritation with "'Lefty.'"

57 RICHARDSON, MAURICE. "James Bond without Fleming." The Ob-
    server (31 March), p. 29.
        Review of Colonel Sun. Amis' attempt to recreate the
    Fleming Bond is unsuccessful for he misses the "cocky sense
    of well-being." While there is some excitement in this
    novel, Bond has become a parody of himself. Amis has tried

1968

to keep him credible and bring him up-to-date, but he has
missed Bond's particular "'ambience.'"

58   SIGGINS, CLARA M. "Fiction." Best Sellers, 28 (15 May), 90.
Review of Colonel Sun. This is "an exciting narrative
with the expertise and verve of Fleming himself." Amis has
added a new dimension to Bond's character--a sensitivity
hidden under his physique.

59   STANLEY, DAVID. "A Flabby Corporate Image for 007." Life,
64 (3 May), 10.
Review of Colonel Sun. Clichés and conventions abound
in this novel. Finds it alarming that Bond's "essential
swinishness is being replaced by some kind of diluted hu-
manism."

60   THOMPSON, JOHN. "An Alphabet of Poets." The New York Review
of Books (1 August), p. 34.
Review of A Look Round the Estate. Amis puts down art,
love, religion, and patriotism, along with all the traditional values of education and the cultured classes. He
promotes sex, autos, and liquor. The language is "deliber-
ately flat and deflated," the form is simple. Amis denies
any "suggestion, mystery, feeling," and because of the simple forms of quatrain or couplet, "the casual daily words
become more than remarks; they become a comment on speech
itself."

61   THORPE, M. "Current Literature: 1967." English Studies, 49
(June), 279.
Brief mention of A Look Round the Estate. Amis' style
is "laconic, hard-shelled."

62   TOMALIN, NICHOLAS. "Amis on Fleming: it takes 40,000 critical
words...." London Sunday Times (25 April), p. 44.
Brief mention and interview on The James Bond Dossier.

63   WIGGIN, MAURICE. "Poetry springing from places." London
Sunday Times (7 January), p. 39.
Review of A Look Round the Estate. A collection of terse
poems of disenchantment, "sometimes savage, always utterly
readable, witty, cerebral."

64   WILSON, DAVID. "Film Reviews." Sight & Sound, 37 (Spring),
99.
Amis advocates a British Force be sent to Vietnam in the
movie Tell Me Lies.

65   ZIMMERMAN, P.D. "Bond Reborn." <u>Newsweek</u>, 71 (6 May), 108.
        Review of <u>Colonel Sun</u>. The novel is unconvincing in
      character, not in details. The voice of experience behind
      the words is unconvincing.

1969 A BOOKS - NONE

1969 B SHORTER WRITINGS

1   ALDISS, BRIAN. "This Listener's Book Chronicle." <u>The Listener</u>,
        65 (23 February), 365.
          Brief mention of <u>New Maps of Hell</u>. Notes Amis' prefer-
      ence for satire over the straight tale of wonder. Calls
      this study informed, balanced, and comprehensive.

2   ALLEN, WALTER. "University Wits," in his <u>The Novel To-day</u>.
        Folcroft, Pennsylvania: The Folcroft Press, pp. 29-31.
          Amis' novels present a "new attitude" and some new val-
      ues in the English novel. He is influenced by the 18th
      century, anti-romantic approach. Says <u>Lucky Jim</u> is the
      funniest novel since <u>Decline and Fall</u>.

3   ANON. "Books." <u>Playboy</u>, 16 (May), 36-38.
          Review of <u>I Want It Now</u>. Says the title of the novel
      refers to what "the Baldocks and their ilk are without:
      tolerance, fair play and decency." Amis makes us laugh
      long and deep like Waugh and Dickens.

4   ANON. "The drunk & the dead." <u>The Times Literary Supplement</u>
        (9 October), p. 1145.
          Review of <u>The Green Man</u>. In the earlier novels, the
      natural world plagued Amis' characters. Now the supernat-
      ural world does, too. Amis combines three genres in this
      novel: ghost story, moral fable, and comic preaching. Of
      these, the ghost story is the least successful because of
      a lack of lingering mystery and spooky atmosphere, and be-
      cause the spirits are there to point a moral and this con-
      fuses us. The greatest pleasure is found in the moral
      fable, for there Amis expresses scorn and contempt for so
      much of life. Concludes that Maurice Allington's loss of
      anxiety about ghosts to engage in sex is also unconvincing.

5   BARTEK, ZENA. "Recent Fiction." London <u>Daily Telegraph</u> (9
        October), p. 23.
          Calls <u>The Green Man</u> a "wrongly weighted novel." Although
      the passages about encounters with ghosts contain some of

1969

the best prose, they lose force "when surrounded by so much farce and irreverence."

6   BROPHY, BRIGID. "The return of Lucky Jim: I Want It Now." The New York Times Book Review (23 May), p. 5.
    Amis' latest novel is weak adult entertainment filled with slang and clichés.

7   CALDER-MARSHALL, ARTHUR. "Unlucky Djinn." London Sunday Telegraph (12 October), p. 20.
    Brief mention of The Green Man. Amis has grown progressively bleaker since Lucky Jim.

8   COLEMAN, JOHN. "Mixed spirits." The Observer (12 October), p. 33.
    Review of The Green Man. From Lucky Jim on, Amis' heroes have been "moral animals." There has been a persistent sense of "the grimness of life or, anyway, of life bound to terminate in death." They try to survive with humor, sex, and practical jokes, often becoming savage with sardonic humor. The Green Man "is most alive in its annotations of ordinary human fraudulences."

9   CONQUEST, ROBERT. "Profile: Robert Conquest discusses Kingsley Amis whose latest novel is published this week." The Listener, 82 (9 October), 485-486.
    A memoir in which Conquest notes a taste for the ribald in Amis. He is, moreover, a skilled versifier of extensive range whose verse combines traditionalism with irreverence. Amis is intensely pro-life, but often too heavily moralistic. Comments on Amis' right-wing political views, also.

10 COOPER, WILLIAM. "Away from this Body." The Listener, 82 (9 October), 489-490.
    Review of The Green Man. As a new departure for Amis, this novel is distinguished by skilled narration, expert construction, and intricate plotting. The use of first person narration allows Amis to incorporate comments in a more interesting and funnier way. Finds a unity of time, for the action occurs in four days. The manifestations of the supernatural are decreasingly haunting, and at the end, Allington reconciles himself to his death.

11 DAVENPORT, GUY. "Elegant Botches." National Review, 21 (3 June), 549.
    Review of I Want It Now. Besides boring in its exposé of the rich, this novel is inconclusive. Amis builds to a

peak, but then leaves off with a weak and disappointing ending.

12 DAVIE, DONALD. "On Hobbits and Intellectuals." Encounter, 30 (October), 87-89, 91.
    Identifies with Amis' right-wing attitudes. Assesses the poem "Masters" as a well-written poem until the last stanza. Says Amis is concerned with the style of authority.

13 DEADMAN, RONALD. "Shaky defence posts." Teachers World (25 April), p. 3.
    Attacks Amis' views on education in Britain.

14 DEMPSEY, DAVID. "Anti-Heel & Non-Heiress." Saturday Review, 52 (5 April), 61.
    Review of I Want It Now. This is not Amis' funniest novel because he tries too hard, ending up with an "anti-heel" and an anti-climax. Amis is not at home with the super-rich. The American characters are stereotypes, and the novel is unconvincing.

15 ELLMAN, MARY. "Recent Novels: The Language of Art." Yale Review, 59 (October), 112-113.
    Review of I Want It Now. Essentially filled with public comment on the world, but "rather funny and quite silly."

16 FREUD, CLEMENT. "Mince ghost." The Spectator, 223 (11 October), 480-481.
    Brief review of The Green Man. Calls it a boring book.

17 GREEN, MARTIN. "Amis and Mailer: the Faustian Contract." Nation, 208 (5 May), 573-574.
    Notes some similarities between Amis and Mailer in temperament and point of view. Their points of view derive from "the experience of evil, of shame, of guilt; the virtues of courage, and honesty, and purposiveness." Their temperament is: "a highly sexed, highly aggressive, irritable, responsible, power-oriented, 'masculine' temperament," unusual in our intellectual climate. Reprinted: 1971.B15.

18 HARTE, BARBARA and CAROLYN RILEY, comps. "Kingsley Amis," in 200 Contemporary Authors. Detroit: Gale, p. 21.
    Brief biographical and bibliographical entry.

19 HARVEY, DAVID D. "Muddle-Browed Fiction." Southern Review, NS 5 (Winter), 267-268.
    Review of The Egyptologists. A satire of sexual warfare and hypocrisy in England. An unsuccessful novel because of

1969

the sense that the writer is participating in the vice
being satirized.

20   HILL, WILLIAM B., S.J. "Fiction." Best Sellers, 29 (1 April),
      9-10.
           Review of I Want It Now. In this novel Amis hasn't lived
      up to the promise of achievement seen in Lucky Jim. Finds
      good satire (as good as Clare Booth Luce's on New York wom-
      en) on television and the rich, and convincing old-fashioned
      romance, but the plot is dull. Except for Simon, the sup-
      porting characters are "paltry;...the character of Simon is
      definite and intriguing."

21   ____. "Fiction: I WIN." America, 120 (3 May), 538.
           Brief review of I Want It Now. Despite a real story
      about conversion, Amis' "animus against the filthy rich"
      poisons the novel.

22   HOPE, FRANCIS. "Sobering." New Statesman, 78 (10 October),
      503-504.
           Review of The Green Man. The novel is more ingenious
      than it is frightening. The voice telling the story is too
      easily recognizable. Finds many laughs and much satire.

23   JELLINEK, ROGER. "Innocents abroad." The New York Times (12
      March), p. 45L.
           Review of I Want It Now. Sees Ronnie as Jim Dixon's
      alter ego. Dixon used faces to defend himself; Ronnie uses
      them to "impress his sincerity like a rubber stamp." For
      most of the novel, Amis barely likes his characters. Be-
      cause of this, the satire is "bad-tempered and irrelevant"
      instead of funny and telling. Also, says the prose is
      wordy and mannered, and the slang is hardly recognizable
      as English.

24   KENNEDY, X.J. "The Devalued Estate." Poetry, 114 (July), 272.
           Review of A Look Round the Estate. In this satirical
      collection, Amis goes in for "candid and often hilarious
      glimpses of such drab gammon-and-eggs life in a Welsh town
      he names Dai Evans country." Notes some similarities to
      Hardy's Satires of Circumstance (the hopeless look at how
      awful life can be if people make it so) and to some of
      Philip Larkin's poems (the theme of frustration).

25   KUEHL, LINDA. "Books: The Poor, the Power Structure, and the
      Polemicist." Commonweal, 90 (16 May), 269-270.
           Review of I Want It Now. Calls the novel a "tour de
      force" of rhetoric depending upon gross clichés for its

effect. Senses that through Ronnie, Amis is venting personal resentment toward the rich. Is an inconsistent novel because Ronnie's conversion at the end isn't foreshadowed.
Notes a shift from irony to sympathy in the portrayal of
Ronnie.

26 LISTER, RICHARD. "Laying the Amis Ghost." London Evening
    Standard (14 October), p. 21.
        Brief mention of The Green Man. Focuses on an analysis
    of Allington's character.

27 MacARTHUR, BRIAN. "Education right wing fights back." London
    Times (5 March), p. 10.
        An account of Black Paper and Amis' comment "more has
    meant worse" in changes in the English educational system.
    Student unrest is due to an academically unfit majority in
    the university, says Amis. To stop giving grades, he adds,
    is to stop educating.

28 MADDOCKS, MELVIN. "An Acid Romance by an Aging 'Angry.'"
    Life, 66 (14 March), 8.
        Review of I Want It Now. Amis develops comedy and a
    "black sense of the ridiculous." The point of view is the
    "disappointed idealist." We clearly see that Amis is re-
    volted by Ronnie and the super-rich. Calls Amis nearly as
    funny as early Waugh, and says this is his best and funniest
    novel since Lucky Jim. Excerpted: 1973.B33.

29 MOON, ERIC. "Fiction." Library Journal, 94 (15 February),
    776.
        Brief review of I Want It Now. A sad book straining for
    humor, filled with clichés and caricature.

30 MORRIS, ROBERT K. "The English Way of Life." Nation, 208
    (28 April), 546.
        Review of I Want It Now. The theme of this novel is the
    need for responsibility in the world. Though Amis' satire
    is consistent, the conversion at the end is ambiguous and
    unconvincing.

31 MORSE, J. MITCHELL. "Brand Names and Others." Hudson Review,
    22 (Summer), 326.
        Review of I Want It Now. Ronnie "is of no human signif-
    icance." The book is of little or no value.

32 OAKES, PHILIP. "Brand New Amis." London Sunday Times (28
    September), p. 61.
        Profile on Amis and The Green Man. Says Amis loathes

1969

all things authoritarian and loves the good life. Amis
says because the press is controlled by the Left, he under-
stands the criticism he receives in the newspapers. What
he writes is prompted by what he reads and likes. Admires
Waugh most of all and calls himself a "congenital mocker."

33   OREL, HAROLD. "The Decline and Fall of a Comic Novelist:
       Kingsley Amis." Kansas Quarterly, 1 (Summer), 17-22.
          Studies the novels through The Anti-Death League, and
       concludes that Amis has declined into an entertainer be-
       cause of commercial success. Lucky Jim was the best be-
       cause in it Amis communicated "the sense of a wholeness of
       man." Also notes that Amis has been losing sympathy with
       his characters. In One Fat Englishman, for example, Amis
       drops several steps below the entertainer we find in Graham
       Greene. Amis' novel is "a story that seldom considers the
       existence of questions other than the old question of what
       comes next."

34   PENNER, ALLEN R. "Human Dignity and Social Anarchy: Sillitoe's
       The Loneliness of the Long-Distance Runner. Contemporary
       Literature, 10 (Spring), 261-262.
          Brief reference to Amis, whose work as one of the "Angry
       Young Men" is quite unlike Sillitoe's novels.

35   PRESS, JOHN. "The Movement and Poets of the 1950's," in his
       A Map of Modern English Verse. New York, London: Oxford
       University Press, p. 253.
          Focuses on Amis' poetry as it relates to the Movement.

36   PRICE, R.G.G. "Book Choice." Punch, 257 (22 October), 681.
          Review of The Green Man. This is a readable and varied
       piece of entertainment. Notes that Amis is unable to re-
       peat himself with each novel. His persona wavers between
       each book. Excerpted: 1973.B33.

37   RASCOE, JUDITH. "Kingsley Amis takes on the Very Rich."
       Christian Science Monitor (10 April), p. 7.
          Review of I Want It Now. In Amis' world, we see how a
       person as cynical, selfish and greedy as Ronnie can deserve
       what he gets. Ronnie learns the art of surviving the whims
       of the wealthy as he learns that the rich are good about
       money and bad about people. Because of the subject, this
       novel is not as funny as the earlier books. For instance,
       the rich have too few conventions to be betrayed for comic
       effect. There is, moreover, very little that's surprising
       about their world. The novel is also weak because of its

"schoolboyish humor," its "coyness in prose," and its com-
plaints (in place of criticism).

*38   RATCLIFFE, MICHAEL. "Two's company, but one's a crowd."
      London Times (11 November), p. v.
         Unlocatable. Listed incorrectly in 1976.A1.

39   ROSS, T.J. "Manners, Morals and Pop: On the Fiction of
      Kingsley Amis." Studies in the Twentieth Century, 4 (Fall),
      61-73.
         Notes an increasing union between popular sentiments and
      gentlemanly manners in Amis' novels. In The Anti-Death
      League, discusses the puzzles hinging on the unraveling of
      characters and events.

40   SCHLEUSSNER, BRUNO. Der neopikareske Roman: Pikareske Ele-
      mente in der Struktur Moderner englischer Romane 1950-1960.
      Bonn: H. Bouvier, pp. 2-5, 204.
         Examines Lucky Jim, Hurry on Down, and Billy Liar as ex-
      amples of the neo-picaresque English novel. Notes that the
      protagonists are anti-heroes in the tradition of the Spanish
      picaro. (In German.)

41   SISSMAN, L.E. "Kingsley Amis at Halfway House." The New
      Yorker, 45 (26 April), 163-170.
         A survey of Amis' novels. Lucky Jim introduced a new
      type of anti-hero to English fiction. Take A Girl Like You
      is the best of all because of its unity of theme and plot,
      depth of characterization, seriousness, intense observations,
      and insights into the sexual relationship. One Fat English-
      man is almost unreadable because of its distaste for the
      hero. The Anti-Death League is weak because it lacks a
      resolution. And I Want It Now is in some ways a return to
      Amis' earlier form. However, the characters are "undiffer-
      ent, two-dimensional, and dull" because of Amis' unrelenting
      hatred for them. Concludes that Amis has "become dislocated
      from his base of knowledge and experience." Excerpted:
      1973.B33.

42   THOMPSON, J.W.M. "Spectator's Notebook." The Spectator, 222
      (28 June), 850.
         Notice recounting Amis' disagreement with the Arts Coun-
      cil over the publication of a list of writers available for
      speaking engagements at colleges. Amis says the fee is too
      small. Sees writers as "important people who make a unique
      contribution to society."

1969

43   TREVOR, WILLIAM. "Funny business." Manchester Guardian (9
     October), p. 9.
          Review of The Green Man. In writing this novel, "only a
     writer as professional as [Amis] could have made of this
     extravagant mixture a book as entertaining and as quietly
     alarming." Maurice is a hypochondriac and womanizer, haunt-
     ed by a ghost, sex and sorcery. Reprinted: 1969.B44.

44   ____. "Funny business." Manchester Guardian Weekly, 101 (18
     October), 18.
          Reprint of 1969.B43.

45   VANN, J. DONN and JAMES T.F. TANNER. "Kingsley Amis: A Check-
     list of Recent Criticism." Bulletin of Bibliography, 26
     (October-December), 105, 111, 115-117.
          Bibliography of secondary sources from 1954 through 1966,
     listed alphabetically by author.

1970 A BOOKS - NONE

1970 B SHORTER WRITINGS

1   ANON. "Kingsley Amis," in The Bibliography of Contemporary
     Poets: 1971. London: Regency Press, p. 11.
          Brief biographical mention and alphabetical listing of
     Amis' poetry collections to 1967.

2   ANON. "Bird netting in Italy 'to win votes.'" London Times
     (16 February), p. 4.
          Note in which Amis protests mass extermination of migra-
     tory birds in Italy as only a vote-getting ploy.

3   ANON. "Books." Playboy, 17 (October), 22-24.
          Review of The Green Man. The novel is a combination of
     sardonic social satire, cool sexual comedy, and horror story.
     Amis gives "back to life some of the mystery that our know-
     it-all culture has tended to erode. The special targets of
     its attack are our numerous life-denying clichés of behav-
     ior and thought."

4   ANON. "Portrait of the artist as a lurcher." The Times Lit-
     erary Supplement (20 November), p. 1349.
          Review of What Became of Jane Austen?. Focuses on sev-
     eral key pieces in this collection. Notes the combination
     of the sense of the ridiculous and of gratitude in the es-
     say on his father and his education. His comments as a
     Fellow reveal the positive side of his attitude toward

education. "Emerges as a man of strong principles and decency who is prepared to query any of the currently accept-
ed highbrow evaluations of the arts." This collection
could be crucial to Amis studies, for it is interesting to
see the changes Amis undergoes.

5   AVANT, J. ALFRED. "Fiction." Library Journal, 95 (July),
      2512.
          Review of The Green Man. Finds the climax unsatisfying.
      Although the evil atmosphere is scary and entertaining, un-
      fortunately Amis allows the "human" element to dominate the
      ending.

6   BELL, PEARL K. "A Tough Act To Follow." New Leader, 53 (21
      September), 17-18.
          Review of The Green Man. Amis is at the top of his form;
      a touching and profound novel whose subject, contemporary
      life, is more than entertaining. Finds that over each nov-
      el, Amis "cast[s] a flare of comic light over subjects he
      obviously takes seriously."

7   BERGONZI, BERNARD. "Kingsley Amis," in his The Situation of
      the Novel. London: MacMillan, pp. 161-174.
          Reprint of 1964.B10 with considerable additions. Finds
      that in fifteen years of writing, Amis' conic spirit dimin-
      ishes to be replaced by an increasing sense of fear and ir-
      rationality. Not just a comic social commentator, Amis is
      also a serious writer with serious concerns. After Lucky
      Jim, which Bergonzi calls "the funniest novel relying
      heavily on linguistic effect," an increased sense of night-
      mare is apparent, until he writes The Anti-Death League,
      his "blackest" novel. Mutual hostility, characters in the
      toils of powerful maligning governing forces, reflect Amis'
      concerns. Excerpted: 1973.B33. Expanded reprint of
      1964.B10.

8   BIĆANIĆ, SONIA. "Cats, Birds and Freedom." Studia Romanica
      et Anglica Zagrebiensia, nos. 29-32, pp. 512-522.
          Studies Dickens' and Amis' differing conceptions of
      freedom and the character's predicament in a corrupt society
      by focusing on two scenes involving cats, birds, and the
      theme of possible freedom in Bleak House and The Anti-Death
      League. Whereas Dickens sees the possibility of individual
      action and resulting good, Amis sees only impotence and
      "the inescapable chemistry of biology, the action of pure
      chance."

1970

9   BURGESS, ANTHONY. "A Racy, Earthy Ghost Story." Life, 66
     (28 August), 11.
           Review of The Green Man. Lately, Amis has been taking a
     popular fictional form and "filling it with his own brand
     of humor and intelligence." Both The Anti-Death League and
     The Green Man "posit the existence of a malign ultimate re-
     ality, against which there is little defense." The Green
     Man is a mixture of humor and a chilling 17th century
     pastiche, all to express a philosophy of stoicism--"the art
     of putting up with things when you can't fight them." Ex-
     cerpted: 1973.B33.

10   COSGRAVE, PATRICK. "Where Amis Stands." London Daily Tele-
     graph (3 December), p. 8.
           In What Became of Jane Austen?, Amis' preference often
     overwhelms his reason. However, he accurately senses "the
     intellectual viciousness of much left-wing political
     thought."

11   DAVENPORT, GUY. "On the Edge of Being." National Review, 22
     (25 August), 903.
           Review of The Green Man. Although the plot is a bit
     contrived and weak, this is still a brilliant comedy of man-
     ners and character, and "a reminder that the English are a
     people unto themselves, and that their sense of the ridic-
     ulous is as robust as ever."

12   DAVIS, L.J. "Ghost story--scary, funny, and sad." Book World
     (13 September), p. 1.
           Review of The Green Man. Amis has left behind the squan-
     dering of his talents in The Anti-Death League, I Want It
     Now, One Fat Englishman, and The Egyptologists to write a
     ghost story which is also a major novel. The dominant nar-
     rative voice is "a highly idiosyncratic, savagely innocent
     point of view" which, like previous voices, expresses "a
     sense of mixed bewilderment and outrage at being trapped
     in the midst of life on earth." However, the novel loses
     focus because it is hard to deal with tender emotions or
     complex personal entanglements, as it is hard to accept
     Amis' protagonist as a wholly sympathetic figure.

13   FIELDHOUSE, HARRY. "Penthouse Interview: Kingsley Amis."
     Penthouse, 2 (October), 35-39, 42.
           Amis comments on political causes, censorship, James
     Bond, sex, versatility as a writer, America, and television
     commentators in this interview.

14 HERNÁDI, MIKLÓS. "Kingsley Amis," in <u>Az angol irodalom a</u>
    <u>huszadik szazadban</u>. Edited by Láslo Báti and Istvan Kristó-
    Nagy. Vol. 2. Budapest: Gondolat, pp. 197-208.
        General survey of Amis' career with particular comments
    on his novels to 1969. (In Hungarian.)

15 HOPE, FRANCIS. "Clever Boy." <u>New Statesman</u>, 80 (27 November),
    725-726.
        Review of <u>What Became of Jane Austen?</u>. Amis is an excel-
    lent descriptive journalist who shifts quickly between moral
    argument and abuse.

16 JONES, D.A.N. "Bumbling." <u>Manchester Guardian</u> (19 November),
    p. 9.
        Review of <u>What Became of Jane Austen?</u>. Amis' essays on
    fiction are valued because Amis has written novels. His
    comments on politics, however, are valueless and pompous.
    Amis gets attention in politics because he is a good poet
    and novelist; he is, however, eccentric and certainly no
    politician.

17 KIELY, ROBERT. "The Green Man." <u>The New York Times Book Re-</u>
    <u>view</u> (23 August), p. 5.
        Review of <u>The Green Man</u>. A "splendid chiller" filled
    with slapstick, parody and satire. The balance between
    laughter and fear contributes to the success of the novel.

18 LEAVIS, F.R. and Q.D. "Bleak House: A Chancery World," in
    their <u>Dickens the Novelist</u>. London: Chatto and Windus,
    p. 141.
        In a brief footnote, compare Amis' social criticism to
    Dickens' and find that Amis denigrates the university lec-
    turer, librarian, man of letters, serious novelist, school-
    master, learned society, and social worker.

19 LEHMANN-HAUPT, CHRISTOPHER. "There Go the Clowns." <u>The New</u>
    <u>York Times</u> (17 August), p. 25.
        Review of <u>The Green Man</u>. Because Maurice is an alcoholic
    and suffering from psychosomatic illness, the novel is "par-
    adoxically a highly credible and nervous-making ghost
    story." Amis' theological joke pulls everything together--
    Maurice's cynicism, the sexual deviations, the jokes about
    religion, art and Englishmen. A highly original novel.

20 LINDERMAN, DEBORAH. "Three English Novels." <u>The Nation</u>, 211
    (5 October), 312-314.
        Review of <u>The Green Man</u>. As a moral fable and horror

1970

tale, the novel is unbalanced. Amis' tone is unclear, and
the novel is lacking in terror.

21 MADDOCKS, MELVIN. "Laugh till he cried." Christian Science
    Monitor (24 September), p. 8.
        Review of The Green Man. Amis demonstrates that like
    Huxley and Waugh, "the funniest young comedians turn into
    the gloomiest old tragedians." What seemed funny when young
    now seems horrible to novelists in their forties. Excerpt-
    ed: 1973.B33.

22 MOYNIHAN, JOHN. "Snuff for the right." London Sunday Tele-
    graph (22 November), p. 10.
        Brief mention of What Became of Jane Austen?.

23 MURDOCH, IRIS. "Existentialists and Mystics," in Essays and
    Poems Presented to Lord David Cecil, edited by W.W. Robson.
    London: Constable, pp. 173-174.
        Distinguishes between the existential novels of Lawrence,
    Hemingway, Sartre and Amis and the mystical novels of Greene,
    Bellow, Spark and Golding.

24 MURPHY, ROSALIE, ed. "Kingsley Amis," in Contemporary Poets
    of the English Language. Chicago and London: St. James
    Press, pp. 19-20.
        Biographical notes and listing of books to 1969.

25 O'FAOLAIN, NUALA. "A comic novelist works an uncongenial me-
    dium." London Times (19 November), p. 15.
        Review of What Became of Jane Austen?. Amis is ineffec-
    tive; "if paranoia powers his fictional satires, if he needs
    to believe that his reading public is mindlessly trendy and
    barely literate, then let us accept the role: may it pro-
    pel him towards many more novels rather than further into
    the essay form."

26 PORTERFIELD, CHRISTOPHER. "Mr. Spleen." Time, 96 (31 August),
    71-73.
        Review of The Green Man. Says the humor dissipates the
    tension and Amis' focus is blurred by too many themes and
    incidents. Maurice, as protagonist, is reminiscent of
    Roger in One Fat Englishman. Credits Amis with the ability
    to encompass God, death and self-loathing without ceasing
    to be funny. The prime comic theme appears to be "mortality
    in all of its implications." Excerpted: 1973.B33.

27   RICKS, CHRISTOPHER. "I was like that myself once." <u>The Lis-</u>
         <u>tener</u>, 84 (26 November), 739-740.
              Brief review of <u>What Became of Jane Austen?</u>. Comments
         on Amis' literary, political and cultural views, saying
         that the scales are falling from his eyes.

28   ROBSON, W.W. "Epilogue: Literature Since 1950," in his <u>Mod-</u>
         <u>ern English Literature</u>. London and New York: Oxford <u>Uni-</u>
         versity Press, p. 154.
              <u>Lucky Jim</u> is typical of 1950's fiction, noted for "its
         businesslike intention to communicate with the reader."
         Finds a focus on human meanness and baseness in this novel
         as well as in the stories in <u>My Enemy's Enemy</u>.

29   _____. "Kingsley Amis as a critic." <u>The Spectator</u>, 225 (28
         November), 690.
              Review of <u>What Became of Jane Austen?</u>. Calls Amis a
         "judicial or evaluative critic" who shows great interest in
         critical principles and whose usual standard is "convincing-
         ness." The autobiographical articles give the "impression
         of a man easily moved to exasperation or grousing, but not
         unkindly."

30   ROSS, ALAN. "Lifting the Elbow." <u>The London Magazine</u>, NS 9
         (January), 119-120.
              Review of <u>The Green Man</u>. An ingenious, convincing ghost
         story and a remarkable study of an aging, heavy-drinking
         middle-class publican. Most fearful of all is the detailed
         account of alcoholic pressure. Excerpted: 1973.B33.

31   RYAN, STEPHEN P. "Fiction." <u>Best Sellers</u>, 30 (1 September),
         209-210.
              Review of <u>The Green Man</u>. This is a new departure for
         Amis. It is a serious novel about the supernatural, much
         in the manner of Charles Williams. However, Amis seems
         unable to decide what kind of novel he is writing. Too
         often the mood of the supernatural is broken up by Maurice
         and his problems, so the links between these two worlds is
         tenuous and unconvincing. The portraits of Maurice and Rev.
         Sonnenschein are particularly memorable, but Amis will still
         always be remembered for <u>Lucky Jim</u>.

32   SISSMAN, L.E. "The Aftermath of Anger." <u>The New Yorker</u>, 46
         (14 November), 204-207.
              Amis is at the top of his form with <u>The Green Man</u>. It
         is both a model ghost story and a very funny commentary on
         fallibility and a makeshift world. Also, Allington is a

1970

> sympathetic character in a frighteningly convincing moral
> parable. "As a ghost story, it is a remarkable book; in
> its humor and humanity, it transcends the genre."

33 SOKOLOV, R.A. "Sylvan Specter." Newsweek, 76 (14 September),
116-118.
> Review of The Green Man. Says the ghost story diminishes
> the great power of the comic opening, forcing Amis from the
> sublime to the ridiculous. Calls the adultery subplot a
> masterpiece of "snide misogyny."

34 STRAUCH, GÉRARD. "Calendar, construction and character in
Kingsley Amis's Lucky Jim." Récherches Anglaises et
Americaines, 3 (March), 58-66.
> Finds a parallel between Dixon's changes of attitude and
> the chronological development of the action in the novel.

35 WEBSTER, HARVEY CURTIS. "War, Cold," in his After the Trauma:
Representative British Novels Since 1920. Lexington: University Press of Kentucky, p. 193.
> The first two novels delighted readers, but there's not
> enough that is new in his later novels.

36 WEEKS, EDWARD. "The Peripatetic Reviewer." Atlantic Monthly,
226 (September), 127.
> Review of The Green Man. Enjoys the character of Maurice,
> for his "cynical, shrewd liveliness" keeps the novel close
> to credible.

37 WILLIAMS, DAVID. "Pieces of Amis." Punch, 259 (18 November),
731.
> Review of What Became of Jane Austen?. The personal
> themes are the best in this collection, for they indicate
> an inch forward to faith. Although a "refreshing, astrin-
> gent book," Amis is very arrogant in the literary, political
> and sociological essays.

38 WILSON, ANGUS. "Right about turn." The Observer (22 November),
p. 30.
> Review of What Became of Jane Austen?. The collection
> is valuable for explaining how Amis has moved so far to the
> right politically. Says much of Amis' protest was aesthetic,
> on behalf of control and in reaction to the modernist move-
> ment in literature. This led to a stand against experimen-
> tal modernists, then journalistic-sociological use of the
> arts, then to culture in the arts, then pop art, and so on.
> Amis made his protest "on behalf of cultural discipline as

part of an assertion of the solid traditional values" of
the middle- and lower-middle classes.

39 YARDLEY, JONATHAN. "After the One Book." The New Republic,
      163 (19 September), 27-28.
        Amis has shown little artistic growth since Lucky Jim.
      His novels are small in scope and emotion, and the source
      of the problem is that Amis doesn't like people very much.
      As a misanthrope, and disliking himself for being one, any
      opportunity for compassion in his work is precluded, and
      thus there is no depth to his fiction. The Green Man is not
      a new departure for Amis. If you've read one Amis book,
      you've read them all. Excerpted: 1973.B33.

40 YVARD, P. "John Wain, révolte et neutralité." Études
      Anglaises, 23 (October-December), 380-394.
        Notes that Amis and Wain have little in common, though
      journalists in the 1950's grouped them together with other
      writers as "Angry Young Men." (In French.)

1971 A BOOKS - NONE

1971 B SHORTER WRITINGS

1 ANON. "Et Al." The New York Times Book Review (19 September),
      p. 36.
        Brief recommendation of What Became of Jane Austen?.
      Says Amis is "crisp, commonsensical, witty, pungent,
      insightful."

2 ANON. "Having it both ways." The Times Literary Supplement
      (24 September), p. 1138.
        Review of Girl, 20. Comments on the "rational morality"
      in the novel, saying that "morality is too grossly grafted
      onto the entertainment." However, Roy's in-search-of-youth
      story should excite pity, terror, and laughs. "Trendiness
      either amuses or exasperates Mr. Amis; but sex and aging
      seriously concern him." Excerpted: 1975.B11.

3 ANON. "Briefly Noted." The New Yorker, 47 (20 November),
      230.
        Review of What Became of Jane Austen?. This is a stim-
      ulating book because most of the essays express views that
      are "heretically unfashionable."

4 BELL, PEARL K. "To provoke a sacred cow." Christian Science
      Monitor (14 October), p. 5.

1971

> Review of What Became of Jane Austen?. Amis is witty,
> inventive, shrewd, and funny. The book is illuminated by
> the same "shrewd comic immunity to cultish cultural epidem-
> ics that distinguish Amis's best novels." Notes that Amis
> advocates common sense and realism.

5   BRADBURY, MALCOLM. The Social Context of Modern English Lit-
erature. New York: Schocken Books, 235 pp., passim.
General remarks about Amis' relation to contemporary
British history.

6   BRAGG, MELVYN. "Class and the Novel." The Times Literary
Supplement (15 October), p. 1262.
Focuses on the rise to privilege of the Amis hero in I
Want It Now. Says Amis needs to be aware of social bound-
aries if he wants to give his characters social context.
Amis attaches his declassé hero to contemporary society,
but overdoes it.

7   BROOKS, JEREMY. "London Ends." London Sunday Times (3 October), p. 41.
Brief review of Girl, 20. The novel is an updated version of "will-she-or-won't-she."

8   CAPEY, ARTHUR. "The Contemporary English Novel," in Literature
and Environment. Edited by Fred Inglis. London: Chatto
and Windus, p. 24.
An assessment of the British postwar novels. Mentions
Amis' novels from Lucky Jim through Take A Girl Like You.

9   CHINNESWARARAO, G.J. "Amis's Take A Girl Like You." Indian
Journal of English Studies, 12 (December), 110-114.
Amis is closer to Fielding than to Richardson on the
subject of sex in Take A Girl Like You; therefore, Patrick
is vindicated.

10 COLLINS, ROSEMARY. "Twixt book and flick." London Sunday
Telegraph (10 January), p. 5.
Amis comments briefly on the adaptation of the novel to
the screen.

11 COLWELL, C. CARTER. "The Twentieth Century: The World Dis-
oriented," in his The Tradition of British Literature. New
York: G.P. Putnam's Sons, p. 371.
Amis, like his contemporaries during the 1950's, attacks
the traditional English values and class rigidity.

12 CRUTTWELL, PATRICK. "Fiction Chronicle." Hudson Review, 24
      (Spring), 177.
          Review of The Green Man. Finds it hard to fit the super-
      natural and Christianity into the rest of the novel. Like
      Graham Greene, Amis shows "the Truth not through a good man,
      but through a ruined man, a contemptible man, and the Truth
      itself will shine all the brighter."

13 FIELD, J.C. "The Literary Scene: 1968-1970-IV." Rêvue Des
      Langues Vivantes, 37 (Winter), 624-625.
          Review of The Green Man. As a "worldly, unsentimental,
      sexually aggressive" man, Maurice is typical of the later
      Amis hero. He is bad for this novel, however, because of
      the problem of credulity or conversion. Maurice accepts the
      ghosts too easily, often taking the supernatural for granted.
      On the other hand, the social satire found in his updating
      the ghost story convention is convincing. The ironic bal-
      ance between the old and the new is occasionally lost be-
      cause of the sexual intrigue.

14 GINDIN, JAMES. "Well Beyond Laughter: Directions From Fifties'
      Comic Fiction." Studies in the Novel, 3 (Winter), 360-361.
          Examines the "pure comic iconoclasm" in Amis' novels
      from Lucky Jim to The Green Man. Because of Amis' special
      comic skill, his comic distance precludes "any sympathetic
      presentation of depth or intensity in human emotions."

15 GREEN, MARTIN. "Amis and Mailer: the Faustian Contract."
      Month, NS 3 (February), 45-48, 52.
          Reprint of 1969.B17.

16 HAMILTON, IAN. "The Making of the Movement." New Statesman,
      81 (23 April), 570.
          Sees New Lines as shallow. Offers Amis' reactions to
      the poetic Movement.

17 HERN, ANTHONY. "Very funny Mr. Amis." London Evening Standard
      (28 September), p. 21.
          Brief mention of Girl, 20. Comments on the plot and
      characterization. This is one of Amis' funniest novels.

18 HIGGINS, JOHN. "Books of the year: Times critics and re-
      viewers make a choice for 1971." London Times (9 December),
      p. 12.
          Girl, 20 is a most entertaining and accurate observation
      of manners of the popular scene. Finds two very sympathetic
      characters in Vandervane and the Furry Barrel.

1971

19   JORDAN, CLIVE. "Knife fighter." New Statesman, 82 (24 Sep-
      tember), 409.
            Review of Girl, 20. Calls this an "unredeemable" book,
      and comments on the "peevish crudity" of a diatribe against
      youth.

20   KAVANAGH, P.J. "Amis's latest lightweight." Manchester Guard-
      ian (24 September), p. 11.
            Review of Girl, 20. Amis attacks senile trend-chasing,
      lust, and the youth scene in this novel. As in his earlier
      works, Amis works off indignations. It is enjoyable be-
      cause it is easy for the reader to share Amis' feelings.
      Beneath, as a moralist, he is advocating the common sense
      approach. Reprinted: 1972.B21.

21   _____. "Clean soup." Manchester Guardian Weekly, 105 (2 Oc-
      tober), 27.
            Reprint of 1971.B20.

22   LARKIN, PHILIP. "Books of the Year." The Observer (19 Decem-
      ber), p. 17.
            Girl, 20 is an "hilarious and literate satire."

23   LEVIN, BERNARD. "Books of the Year." The Observer (19 Decem-
      ber), p. 17.
            Girl, 20 is a funny, moving novel, "more searching in
      its revelation of human truth than almost anything he has
      written."

24   LODGE, DAVID. "Chapter 7," in his The Novelist at the Cross-
      roads and Other Essays on Fiction and Criticism. New York:
      Cornell University Press, p. 20.
            It is difficult to reconcile Amis' absorption with
      Fleming (in The James Bond Dossier) with his stance as nov-
      elist and critic in the 1950's as "defender of a traditional
      kind of literary realism." In Colonel Sun, for instance,
      Amis takes a "holiday from realism," though the novel is
      more realistic than Fleming's. This is because Bond survives
      by his wits and luck rather than gadgetry. Excerpted:
      1973.B33.

25   McGUINNESS, FRANK. "Yawning Chasms," The London Magazine,
      NS 10 (December-January), 159-162.
            Review of Girl, 20. The humor is like early Amis, but
      unfortunately the caustic commentary on the present social
      scene "degenerates into a kind of 'Disgustedly yours'-type
      tirade against those who do not happen to share his par-
      ticular taste and prejudice." Still, this is an entertaining

and encouraging book for those who believe we should widen the generation gap. Excerpted: 1973.B47.

26 MacLEOD, NORMAN. "This familiar regressive series: Aspects of Style in the Novels of Kingsley Amis," in <u>Edinburgh Studies in English and Scots</u>. Edited by A.J. Aitken <u>et al</u>. London: Longman, pp. 121-143.
   Studies Amis' style in his first five novels and seeks to define some of the sources and functions of comedy in the novels. Notes that the novels are held together by repetition, cross-reference, and an easily identifiable Amis hero who has a private language of his own. Very often, he says, "the source of comedy lies in the use of language" by both Amis and his characters acting in the novels. "It is not in comic linguistic oddity, obtrusive and obvious, that Amis's style resides but in a teasing, playing around with language where not only is there no obtrusive oddity but, in fact, where expressions emerge that must be admitted as lexically acceptable and grammatical forms of English."

27 MOON, ERIC. "Literature." <u>Library Journal</u>, 96 (15 September), 2773.
   Review of <u>What Became of Jane Austen?</u>. Calls the study "something of an anthology of perversity" and "a self-revealing picture of Amis' success-slide into reaction." Mourns for the amiable Amis of <u>Lucky Jim</u>.

28 MOYNIHAN, JOHN. "Musical chairs." London <u>Sunday Telegraph</u> (26 September), p. 22.
   Brief favorable mention of <u>Girl, 20</u>.

29 PRITCHARD, WILLIAM H. "The Current State of Criticism." <u>Hudson Review</u>, 24 (Winter), 704-705.
   Review of <u>What Became of Jane Austen?</u>. Gives general praise for Amis' essays on Keats, Thomas, Cambridge, and Leslie Fieldler. Amis is "humane, literate, and witty."

30 RATCLIFFE, MICHAEL. "A caper round the cultural abyss." London <u>Times</u> (27 September), p. 11.
   Review of <u>Girl, 20</u>. Notes an edge of terror to the conflict between Vandervane and Yandell "that gives the novel a darker flavour than might have been deduced from its exceptionally high entertainment-value alone." Vandervane exemplifies "radical chic," and Yandell's consciousness informs the novel. Through them, Amis attacks irresponsibility and laments lost certainties in this "black comedy."

1971

31   SAMPSON, ANTHONY. "Books of the Year." The Observer (19 De-
      cember), p. 17.
           Praises Girl, 20 and says the "character of Sir Roy
      Vandervane is a genuinely new, comic creation."

32   SCOTT, MICHAEL MAXWELL. "Pressed into slaving." London Daily
      Telegraph (30 September), p. 13.
           Calls Girl, 20 "a casual romp." "Amis never fails to
      amuse with his turn of phrase and oblique, comic
      characterisation."

33   SEYMOUR, WILLIAM KEAN. "Concern For Literature." Contemporary
      Review, 218 (February), 109.
           Review of What Became of Jane Austen?. Amis displays
      "cogent thinking, direct and humorous observation and schol-
      arly control of language which never becomes pedantic."

*34   SUMMERS, JOHN. The Rag Parade. London: New English Library.
           Unlocatable. Listed in 1976.A1. Unfavorable memoir of
      one of Amis' former Swansea students.

35   THEROUX, PAUL. "Professional writer." Book World (17 October),
      p. 8.
           Review of What Became of Jane Austen?. After a short
      discussion of the differences between American and British
      writers, Theroux says this is "a chronicle of a writer's
      changing concerns rather than a detailed discussion of the
      concerns themselves."

36   THOMAS, EDWARD. "The English Cramp." The London Magazine, NS
      10 (February)´, 90-93.
           Review of What Became of Jane Austen?. Notes many pos-
      itive qualities in this collection, particularly his style,
      openings, retractions, interests in the thriller, hilarity,
      and attack on Lawrence. Disagrees with Amis' attack on the
      Lefties and his "note of hysteria."

37   TOYNBEE, PHILIP. "Old goat, young bitch." The Observer (26
      September), p. 37.
           Review of Girl, 20. From Lucky Jim to Girl, 20 there is
      a development from farce to a highly professional satire.
      In his latest novel, the two central characters are observed
      rather than acted upon by Yandell. Comments on Amis' ten-
      derness and indulgence for Vandervane; like earlier char-
      acters, his "frankness is more than enough to atone for
      [his] folly." However, there is no sympathy for Sylvia,
      whom Toynbee calls "a monster." Because Sylvia becomes

unbelievable, if the purpose of Amis' satire is "to arouse
<u>and sustain</u> the readers' indignation," then the book fails.

38   TURNER, E.S. "The New Amis." <u>The Listener</u>, 86 (23 September),
         407.
            Review of <u>Girl, 20</u>. The characters are creatures of the
         media, exemplifying youth vs. middle age. Despite its sad-
         ness and pessimism, the novel is exceedingly funny and typ-
         ical of Amis at his best.

39   TURNILL, OSCAR. "Watch it, mate." London <u>Sunday Times</u> (9
         May), p. 31.
            Brief mention of <u>The Importance of Being Hairy</u>. Includes
         a summary of contents and a commentary on its relation to
         Amis' other works.

40   WILSON, COLIN. "Quip Counter Quip." <u>The Spectator</u>, 227 (30
         October), 623-624.
            Review of <u>Girl, 20</u>. Amis' problem is how to be a sati-
         rist while at the same time espouse an anti-intellectual
         position. He has not quite accomplished this in his latest
         novel. Notes a somber view of society beneath the humor
         and objects to the musical opinions of the narrator.

41   ZAVARZADEH, MAS'UD. "Anti-Intellectual Intellectualism in the
         Postwar English Novel." <u>Ball State University Forum</u>, 12
         (Autumn), 68-73.
            Amis, among others, is known for his reaction against
         literary modernism. <u>Lucky Jim</u> struck a new note in the anti-
         modernist movement in English literature. Zavarzadeh traces
         the roots of "cultivated philistinism and its deliberately
         anti-intellectual approach."

1972 A BOOKS

1   SOLSTAD, KENNETH de FOREST. "Role Playing in the Fiction of
         Kingsley Amis." Ph.D. dissertation, University of California
         at Berkeley.
            A transactional analysis of Amis' novels.

1972 B SHORTER WRITINGS

1   ANON. "English and American." <u>Choice</u>, 8 (January), 1148.
            <u>The Green Man</u> is weak and unsatisfying.

1972

2   ANON. "Literature." Booklist, 68 (1 January), 376.
     Brief mention of What Became of Jane Austen?.

3   ANON. "Books." Playboy, 19 (February), 28.
     Review of Girl, 20. The most distinctive feature is "its
     muzzled sympathy for its subject." By the end, our sympa-
     thies are caught by Vandervane rather than by Yandell.
     "Amis proves he can be as funny tilting at youth as tilting
     at the establishment."

4   ANON. "Briefly Noted." The New Yorker, 47 (5 February), 102-
     103.
     Review of Girl, 20. An entertaining novel. Amis has
     never been funnier or more serious.

5   ANON. "Fiction." Booklist, 68 (15 February), 487.
     Review of Girl, 20. Says the novel contains some farce
     and some elements of social criticism.

6   ANON. "Notes On Current Books." Virginia Quarterly Review,
     48 (Spring), lii.
     Review of Girl, 20. A surprising novel as Amis parodies
     today's life-styles with bitter humor without being preachy.
     Amis is back in form with this novel.

7   ANON. "English and American." Choice, 9 (July), 642.
     Review of What Became of Jane Austen?. An important book
     because it gives insight into the person of Amis. Ranges
     from clever to impertinent, somber to funny.

8   ANON. "Bookend." The Spectator, 229 (8 July), 57.
     Comments on Amis' job as a booze reviewer for Penthouse.

9   ANON. "Bookend." The Spectator, 229 (2 September), 365.
     Gives the story behind the cover picture for On Drink.

10   ANON. "In favour." The Times Literary Supplement (15 Decem-
     ber), p. 1525.
     Brief mention of G.K. Chesterton: Selected Stories.

11   ANON. "Drink." The Times Literary Supplement (22 December),
     1566.
     Review of On Drink. Although a funny book of practical
     value, "the bright jolliness that can be carried off in an
     article palls on the colder pages of a book."

12   ANON. "Forking Out." The Economist, 245 (30 December), 73.
     Review of On Drink. Comes in handy during that time

when a man can't think of what to drink. Notes a few
inaccuracies.

13   BOSTON, RICHARD. "Writers at Work." <u>New Statesman</u>, 84 (6 October), 480-481.
    Review of <u>What Became of Jane Austen?</u>. Amis upholds de-
cency, tolerance, and reason. His essays become increasingly
predictable.

14   BRADBURY, MALCOLM. "The Novel," in <u>The Twentieth Century Mind:
Volume III</u>. Edited by C.B. Cox and A.E. Dyson. New York
and London: Oxford University Press, pp. 331, 337, 340-
341, 344.
    Comments on the "moral realism" in <u>Lucky Jim</u> and the men-
tion of Henry Fielding in <u>I Like It Here</u>. Sees a similarity
between the comedy of Fielding and Amis in <u>I Want It Now</u>.
In Amis, "the hero is usually the hero by virtue of his
identification with the system of linguistic preferences
embodied in the novel."

15   BROYARD, ANATOLE. "A Case of How It Strikes You." <u>The New
York Times</u> (6 January), p. 35.
    Review of <u>Girl, 20</u>. A funny novel whose "effects are
derived mostly from its characters, who are all recognizable
contemporary types."

16   CASSILL, R.B. "A distaste for permissiveness, a taste for
cool: <u>Girl, 20</u>." <u>The New York Times Book Review</u> (16 January), p. 7.
    Review of <u>Girl, 20</u>. Amis adapts the old moral fable about
Pied Piper to a contemporary novel to express his distaste
for permissiveness and its consequences. Says his satire
is enriched by ambiguities. "The message is Spenglerian,
but the mood remains spritely."

17   COOK, BRUCE. "Ha Ha! Ho Ho! But Wait a Sec: Is Mr. Amis
Serious After All?" <u>The National Observer</u> (29 January),
p. 23.
    Review of <u>Girl, 20</u>. The fact that Amis performs so well
at more than entertainment has proved his undoing. In the
early novels, it is easy to be amused without worrying much
about the gradual "deepening and darkening" of his work.
Moreover, Amis' passion for popular literature seemed to
indicate he felt the same way about the level of his work.
With <u>The Anti-Death League</u>, however, there is a problem.
Many readers saw it as a game of lively espionage à la Ian
Fleming and John Le Carré. Few saw the novel as "an effort
to carry the spy game to its logical conclusions, to come

1972

to grips with the eschatological questions that were implicit in it." Similarly, The Green Man was read as just a ghost story and not the perplexing metaphysical novel it is. And, until the last chapter of Girl, 20, the novel may look like a return to Lucky Jim. But the ending develops logically from all the foolishness before it, to express the theme "no matter how funny its parts, life is a tragic whole." Concludes that it is time readers realize Amis has dealt with problems of this magnitude for some time.

18   COOPER, ARTHUR. "A Look at Some Recent Novels." Newsweek, 79 (6 March), 77.
Brief review of Girl, 20. Calls it "a first rate, wonderfully funny" novel.

19   COOPER, DEREK. "Knocking it back." Manchester Guardian Weekly, 107 (9 December), 20.
Review of On Drink. Notes a combination of misanthropic vein and serious advice with humor in this book. Amis "has been taking the starch out of those who write fatuously on wine" for some time.

20   DEGNAN, JAMES P. "Fiction Chronicle." Hudson Review, 25 (Summer), 330-337.
In the early novels, Amis was "the scourge of an establishment long overdue for a scourging." Amis overturned the tradition of the sensitive, alienated young hero struggling in a rough, middle-class materialistic world by making the hero a villain. Since then, Amis' work has declined in quality. Girl, 20 is the worst. In it, Amis is indifferent to telling a good story. The problem begins for Amis with Take A Girl Like You, wherein the Lucky Jim type of hero begins to become a kind of anti-hero, so that Amis loses the moral core of his earlier comic satires. In the early novels, Amis' satire "offers us a clear alternative to what is being attacked." In Girl, 20, however, Douglas Yandell is a half-hearted, trivial character. Little else is offered as an alternative, and, unlike the earlier works, the object of satire is of only peripheral concern to Yandell. Excerpted: 1973.B33.

21   DeVITIS, A.A. Anthony Burgess. Twayne English Authors Series, edited by Sylvia E. Bowman. Boston: Twayne Publishers, pp. 26, 29, 79.
Burgess defines the anti-hero in Lucky Jim. Although Dixon asks little from life, he can't even have that. Eventually he marries above himself.

120

22   DRIVER, CHRISTOPHER. "Mean Sods." The Listener, 88 (7 December), 801-802.
        Review of On Drink. In this disappointing book, Amis comments on such subjects as wine, hangovers, and mixed drinks. Driver includes an anecdote of having drinks with Amis.

23   FORREST, ALAN. "b & b's look at 1971." Books & Bookmen, 17 (February), 26-27.
        Cites Girl, 20 as the worst book of the year.

24   GINDIN, JAMES. "Kingsley Amis," in Contemporary Novelists. Edited by James Vinson. New York: St. Martin's Press, pp. 44-48.
        Brief biographical sketch with bibliographical summary.

25   GRAVER, LAURENCE. "Saturday Review Books." Saturday Review, 55 (15 January), 43-44.
        Review of What Became of Jane Austen?. This is a masterly example of "cant detection." Finds a more persuasive judgment in the autobiographical essays, for Amis comes to a fuller understanding of people and events than he attains when dealing with books.

26   HAIMART, S.M. "Lucky Jim ou la tunique de Nessus." Études Anglaises, 25 (July-September), 367-384.
        A detailed summary of Amis' career as critic, novelist and poet. (In French.)

27   HOPE, FRANCIS. "Mourning After." New Statesman, 84 (1 December), 812.
        Review of On Drink. Calls Amis "a moralist with a slight dash of hedonism."

28   HUTCHINSON, H.E. "Fiction." Library Journal, 97 (1 April), 1344.
        Review of Girl, 20. An unsuccessful novel because it's hard to care for the main character. He is not nice and he is two-dimensional.

29   JONES, D.A.N. "Brown Studies." The Listener 88 (26 October), 557.
        Brief mention of G.K. Chesterton: Selected Stories. Says Amis has much in common with Chesterton as a polemical poet-novelist.

30   KELLY, EDWARD. "Satire and Word Games in Amis's Englishman." Satire Newsletter, 9 (Spring), 132-138.

1972

Because Amis often seems out of touch with current American diction, and because his jokes pivot on obscure Britishisms, "his American frequently sounds British, confusion blunts the satire, and targets become ambiguous" in One Fat Englishman. Says Roger emerges an endearing and sympathetic character among a pack of disgusting Americans.

31 KERMODE, FRANK. "The British Novel Lives." Atlantic Monthly, 230 (July), 88.
Review of Girl, 20. Comments on the sad state of the novel and the literary scene in England, then says it is hard to describe the tone of Girl, 20 because it is a combination of laughs, sourness, and tragedy. Like The Anti-Death League, it is more serious than it sounds.

32 LEMON, LEE T. "Some English Fiction." Prairie Schooner, 46 (Fall), 268.
Review of Girl, 20. Reminiscent of Lucky Jim with its humor, but offers a more mature insight into the Lucky Jim kind of man in Douglas Yandell. "There is a very wise author lurking behind his shallowly intelligent hero."

33 McDOWELL, FREDERICK P.W. "Recent British Fiction: Some Established Writers." Contemporary Literature, 11 (Autumn), 405-406.
Review of I Want It Now. As an exposé of the arrogant rich and their exploitation of power, this is an amusing and interesting novel. Although sympathy is aroused for Ronnie and Simon, Ronnie's character is contrived.

34 _____. "Time of Plenty: Recent British Novels." Contemporary Literature, 13 (Summer), 366-368.
Review of The Green Man and Girl, 20. The Green Man is excellent for its pacing, structure, setting, characterization and use of the supernatural. Sees Allington as an Everyman. In Girl, 20, Amis is more sardonic in tone. Because neither Roy nor Yandell can communicate meaningfully with others, their devotion to music is suspect and Amis' view of the sterile contemporary cultural scene is "faintly terrifying."

35 MANO, D. KEITH. "Enormous Trifles." National Review, 24 (14 April), 408-409.
Review of Girl, 20. An insignificant work in which Amis tries to mix Wodehouse's style with Waugh's aspirations. Amis favors the traditional virtues, both societal and musical.

36   MAY, DERWENT. "Amis, McCarthy, Naipaul." Encounter, 38 (Jan-
        uary), 74-75.
            Review of Girl, 20. Notes a problem with narration. In
        I Want It Now, Ronnie was implausible because of the abrupt
        conversion. The Green Man was unconvincing because the tone
        alternated. Girl, 20 stresses the importance of sexual sat-
        isfaction, and while crudeness and irresponsibility are as-
        sociated with this, Amis seems to be appealing for sexual
        realism. This problem, thus, stems from Amis' irresolution
        about how to relate the moral and sexual drives.

37   MECKIER, JEROME. "Looking Back at Anger: The Success of A
        Collapsing Stance." The Dalhousie Review, 52 (Spring), 47-
        58.
            Shows that Lucky Jim is more complex than just an out-
        burst against an unfair social order. Rather, it is a study
        of the futility of anger and its inadequacies and "eventual
        collapse as an approach to life." Dixon is transformed as
        he learns that anger is not a self-sufficient way of life.

38   MORRIS, DENIS. "Wines To Delight In." London Daily Telegraph
        (30 November), p. 13.
            On Drink is a "slender book of proportionate appeal."

39   MOYNIHAN, JOHN. "My Book of The Year--II." London Sunday
        Telegraph (2 January), p. 20.
            Cites Girl, 20 as book of the year.

40   MUGGERIDGE, MALCOLM. "Books." Esquire, 77 (January), 30.
            Brief mention of What Became of Jane Austen?. Amis is
        "a sprightly essayist," often "amusing, deft and sagacious."

41   OBERBECK, S.K. "Birds in hand and head." Book World, 9 (9
        January), 4.
            Review of Girl, 20. This is a disappointing book, for
        it is too late to deal with trendy people and "fashion, fad,
        and spiritual poverty." The characters are somewhat super-
        ficial, the humor is broad, and the plot is leisurely. Po-
        tentially interesting characters, such as Lothario, Harold
        Meers, and Sylvia, are underdeveloped. By the end, the
        novel dwindles into Wodehouse "with a social uplift and some
        ideological ire, but it's too late."

42   RICKS, CHRISTOPHER. "Youth and Asia." The New York Review of
        Books (9 March), pp. 23-25.
            Review of Girl, 20. Comparable to Bharati Mukherjee's
        The Tiger's Daughter in its picture of the generation gap,
        its "certain smugness," and its literary allusions of the

1972

university teacher of English. "In Amis's England, it is
the unruliness of sexual desire, coupled with the brisk fea-
sibility of promiscuity, that so complicates the conflict
between the generations." Says the irony and quandary "are
such as to elicit from him here much that is shrewd, fretful,
and lugubriously funny, founded upon self-scrutiny and not
self-regard."

43   RILEY, CAROLYN. "Fiction." Best Sellers, 31 (1 February),
      473-474.
           Review of Girl, 20. Amis is primarily interested in the
      behavior of the individual rather than the characteristics
      of their differing social classes. Notes again the mixture
      of "realism, absurdity, grotesquerie, and fairy tale as back-
      ground." However, at the center there is still no profound
      philosophical or psychological principle at work. Amis'
      satire is "unleavened," to become weak and lacking in cred-
      ibility, and his narrative becomes "precious, coy, and
      insipid."

44   S., P.H. "All the Dirt." London Times (7 January), 12.
           In a news item, Yevgeni Yevtushenko attacks Amis for his
      anti-Soviet pronouncements and support for the Vietnam war.

45   SCHLEUTER, PAUL. "Girl, 20." Saturday Review, 55 (15 January),
      35-36.
           Review of Girl, 20. Finds an undercurrent of "pathos,
      darkness, and trauma," as he explores Vandervane's foolish
      desires to regain his youth and Yandell's difficulties as
      a moderating influence on both Vandervane and his wife.
      Girl, 20 is a "more mature examination of human foibles and
      excesses than was the case in his earlier novels."

46   SHEPPARD, R.A. "Butter on the Bow." Time, 99 (7 February),
      88.
           Review of Girl, 20. The plot is fairly complex and far-
      cical, but it is a shallow novel. "Only Amis' talent as a
      storyteller and stylist keeps Girl, 20 from settling into
      the pettiest smugness."

47   SWINDEN, PATRICK. "English Poetry," in The Twentieth Century
      Mind: Volume III. Edited by C.B. Cox and A.E. Dyson. New
      York and London: Oxford University Press, p. 387.
           In "Against Romanticism," Amis mocks the "combination of
      pretension and obscurity, the claims to mysterious knowl-
      edge and the inability (so it is claimed) to produce the
      evidence for it."

48 VOORHEES, RICHARD J. "Kingsley Amis: Three Hurrahs and a
    Reservation." Queen's Quarterly, 79 (Spring), 38-46.
        Recognizes the enormous range of Amis, but suggests that
    Amis may have dissipated his talents as well as developed
    them. Colonel Sun is an absurd formula mixture of sex and
    sadism, moralizing, food snobbery, pedantry and redundance.
    The Anti-Death League is a thriller, but the materials are
    too disparate to be integrated. The first three novels, how-
    ever, are fun, and Lucky Jim is a first-rate comic novel.
    The early heroes are uncomfortable among intellectual and
    cultural matters. They seek a distinction between genuine
    and fake, and are essentially good men. Like Fielding, Amis
    demonstrates comic skill, moral seriousness, and simplicity.
    Concludes that although Amis has experimented, matured, and
    in many ways become more substantial and significant, his
    early works are "purer satisfactions."

49 WORDSWORTH, CHRISTOPHER. "Bacchus and pards." The Observer
    (3 December), p. 40.
        Review of On Drink. "A stirring practical guide to the
    hazards and rewards of drinking."

1973 A BOOKS - NONE

1973 B SHORTER WRITINGS

1   ADAMS, PHOEBE. "Short Reviews: Books." Atlantic Monthly,
    232 (October), 130.
        Review of The Riverside Villas Murder. This is a spoof
    on the detective novel. The motives and methods are ridic-
    ulous, and the eccentric detective is irrelevant.

2   ALLEN, TREVOR. "books in brief." Books & Bookmen, 18 (June),
    138.
        Brief mention of On Drink.

3   ANON. "Commentary." The Times Literary Supplement (23 Feb-
    ruary), p. 210.
        Review of Tennyson, Selected by Kingsley Amis. Comments
    on Amis' judicious but short introduction to Tennyson. Says
    the selections are original.

4   ANON. "Small town murder." London Daily Express (5 April),
    p. 17.
        Brief mention of The Riverside Villas Murder. Amis ef-
    fectively captures the 1930's era.

1973

5   ANON. "That Amis bloke's having a smack at whodunits." London
     Daily Mail (4 April), p. 7.
          Brief mention of The Riverside Villas Murder with plot
     summary.

6   ANON. "The turns of a plain man." The Times Literary Supple-
     ment (6 April), pp. 393-394.
          Review of The Riverside Villas Murder. Says the changes
     in Amis' work can be understood in relation to his changes
     in attitude to life and society. In Girl, 20, he coordi-
     nates for the first time "his tastes, his theme and his
     talents." Comments on the fun, shaky plot, realistic char-
     acterization and period detail in The Riverside Villas Mur-
     der. Excerpted: 1975.B11.

7   ANON. "Onward, Cultural Soldiers." The Economist, 247 (5 May),
     Spring Book Survey Supplement, 5-6.
          Review of The Riverside Villas Murder. This is an ex-
     ploration of "what happens to adolescents faced for the
     first time with that loss of faith in the adult-as-hero that
     both abets and destroys youthful fantasy," more so than
     Agatha Christie or Margery Allingham ever could manage. The
     novel is entertaining, absorbing, and thought-provoking.

8   ANON. "Fiction." Kirkus, 41 (1 July), 698.
          Review of The Riverside Villas Murder. Although the crime
     story is weak, the novel is worth reading for its good humor,
     likeability of Peter, and characterization of Col. Manton.
     Calls this a "bit of cheerful nostalgia."

9   ANON. "Mystery and Suspense." Publishers' Weekly, 204 (23
     July), 64.
          Brief review of The Riverside Villas Murder. Amis' re-
     creation of a 1930's period atmosphere is "authentic and
     amusing." This is "sophisticated and witty fun for Amis
     fans."

10   ANON. "One Pickle butty." London Sun (7 August), p. 5.
          Brief mention of Amis' favorite sandwich.

11   ANON. "Nonfiction." Publishers' Weekly, 204 (13 August), 54.
          Brief review of On Drink. This is a witty, pleasant
     "aperitif."

12   ANON. "Non-fiction." Kirkus, 41 (15 August), 916.
          Brief mention of On Drink. Amis pays attention to the
     smallest detail in this book.

1973

13 ANON. "Craven Amis." The Listener, 90 (6 September), 310.
     Comments on Amis' views on The Riverside Villas Murder
   (as an historical novel), Wesker and Lessing, boys and sex.

14 ANON. "Briefly Noted: Fiction." The New Yorker, 49 (8 October), 169-170.
        Brief review of The Riverside Villas Murder. Somewhat
   a parody with humor and "affectionate understanding."

15 ANON. "English and American." Choice, 10 (November), 1378-1379.
        Brief mention of Tennyson, Selected by Kingsley Amis.
   The selections are unexpected.

16 ANON. "Classified Books." Booklist, 70 (15 December), 410-411.
        Brief review of On Drink. This is a delightful guide
   distinguished by bright wit and an eye for enjoyment and
   economy.

17 NO ENTRY.

18 ARLOTT, JOHN. "Books for imbibers." Manchester Guardian (1 March), p. 11.
        Brief mention of On Drink.

19 BLUMBERG, MYRNA. "Amis: nostalgia for the thirties." London Times (5 April), p. 16.
        Review of The Riverside Villas Murder. Amis is in top
   form. "He never seriously took on that mystery story, and
   here he has perfected the very civil art of not overworking
   his readers but making me want more, now."

20 BOLD, ALAN. "Literature: Hot-Line To the Muse." The Times Educational Supplement (9 March), p. 23.
        Brief mention of Tennyson, Selected by Kingsley Amis.
   The collection gives us insight into Amis and his own work.

21 BROOK, STEPHEN. "The best ways to get and get rid of a hangover: On Drink." The New York Times Book Review (23 December), p. 9.
        Brief mention of On Drink.

22 BROOKS, JEREMY. "Child's play." London Sunday Times (8 April), p. 39.
        Review of The Riverside Villas Murder. The novel has the

1973

feel "of immediate, beautifully observed, personal experience." The detail is perfect. Because of the 14-year-old point of view, it is logical to deal with the subject of sex, too. Few contemporary writers are "as touchingly funny and as drily matter-of-fact as Kingsley Amis."

23 BROYARD, ANATOLE. "Ho Hum Mayhem." The New York Times (26 September), p. 39L.
     Review of The Riverside Villas Murder. Whereas Girl, 20 is one of Amis' wittiest novels, this is "slow, mildly boring, improbable and mechanically tricked-out." Concludes that Amis' sense of irony is working against him.

24 CAREY, JOHN. "The Captain and the Colonel." The Listener, 89 (5 April), 457.
     Review of The Riverside Villas Murder. The 1930's setting makes the "horrid horrider." This, together with the dreamy side of life between wars, captures the reader's attention. Distinguished by Peter's sex life, the novel is an intricate whodunit and a "loving model of 1936 tennis club suburbia."

25 CARR, JOHN DICKSON. "Sound Lad." New Statesman, 86 (6 April), 497.
     Review of The Riverside Villas Murder. Praises the authentic 1930's atmosphere. Amis has mastered the techniques of detective fiction. "The story grips, holds, and won't let go."

26 COLE, WILLIAM. "Feece and Pear?" World, 2 (14 August), 35.
     Brief mention of On Drink and The Riverside Villas Murder. On Drink is too British to appeal to the American reader, whereas the detective novel is a good thriller, but there is some problem with many of the Britishisms left in.

27 COSGRAVE, PATRICK. "The Pleasure of Murder." World, 2 (8 May), 42-44.
     Review of The Riverside Villas Murder. The numerous clues and splendid rationalization of the murder invites comparison with the masters. Offers comments on what is happening to the detective novel today. Says Col. Manton remains to be fully developed. Excerpted: 1975.B11.

28 de FEO, RONALD. "Fiction Chronicle." Hudson Review, 26 (Winter), 781-782.
     Review of The Riverside Villas Murder. This marks the decline of a first-rate comic writer. The semi-serious, realistic story of Peter contrasts sharply with the "playful,

unrealistic, 'literary' murder story," and this becomes frus-
trating for the reader. Moreover, the sexual adventures are
a padding for the mystery story.

29 DUECK, JACK. "Uses of the Picaresque: A Study of Five Modern
    British Novels." Ph. D. dissertation, University of Notre
    Dame.
        "In Lucky Jim, the uses of masking and puppetry serve as
    metaphors for the chameleon nature of the world and the cor-
    responding need for protean behaviour. The counterpoint to
    the picaro is introduced through picaresque elements." The
    picaresque traits both "dramatize the chaotic world while
    prodding the protagonist, by accident or luck, toward a non-
    picaresque discovery of life." Besides Lucky Jim, also com-
    ments on Hurry on Down, Under the Net, Herself Surprised,
    and Murphy.

30 GRUENROCK, FRIEDA. "Home At The Range." Best Sellers, 33 (15
    November), 384.
        Brief mention of On Drink. Calls it amusing, informative,
    even sensible.

31 HANSON, HENRY. "Hangover Helpers and Bathtub Booze." Panorama,
    Chicago Daily News (17-18 November), p. 10.
        Brief mention of On Drink. Finds it entertaining and
    varied. The hangover advice is especially appealing.

32 HOLLOWAY, DAVID. "Recent Fiction." London Daily Telegraph
    (5 April), p. 8.
        Brief mention of The Riverside Villas Murder.

33 JAMES, CLIVE. "Books of the Year." The Observer (16 December),
    p. 33.
        Cites The Riverside Villas Murder as best novel of the
    year.

34 KALEM, T.E. "Club Pro at Work." Time, 102 (10 September), 92-
    94.
        Brief review of The Riverside Villas Murder. A "mild
    parody" in which Amis combines two British literary forms,
    the mystery thriller and the boyhood adventure yarn. Ex-
    cerpted: 1975.B11.

35 KIRSCH, ROBERT. "The Book Report: Mystery Era Re-Created."
    The Los Angeles Times (17 September), part IV, p. 7.
        Review of The Riverside Villas Murder. Amis captures the
    golden age of mystery and succeeds in his recreation of the

1973

old form. Col. Manton is a descendant of Sherlock Holmes.
Finds many surprises in plot and character.

36   MAKIMS, VIRGINIA. "Full of Clues." The Times Educational Sup-
      plement (29 June), p. 25.
            Brief review of The Riverside Villas Murder. Amis pre-
      sents a superb gallery of characters in this "readable and
      entertaining" novel.

37   MOON, ERIC. "Cookery." Library Journal, 98 (1 September),
      2440.
            Favorable review of On Drink. "Literate, lively, funny
      as hell."

38   NYE, ROBERT. "Murder by Kingsley Amis." Books & Bookmen, 18
      (May), 80-81.
            Review of The Riverside Villas Murder. This is a liter-
      ary pleasure because all of the detective story ingredients
      are here. The secret of its success lies in the fact that
      Amis likes his two central characters, Peter and Col. Manton.
      Each is a variant of the Amis hero. Moreover, the sexual
      tension between Peter and the Colonel is a motivating factor
      in the solution to the murder.

39   _____. "Textures of time." Manchester Guardian (5 April),
      p. 4.
            Review of The Riverside Villas Murder. Amis recreates
      the period of the 1930's in every detail. If read analyt-
      ically, it is easy to detect the killer. More interesting
      than that, however, is the degree to which it is an exercise
      in detective fiction. A clever book with a "crisp air of
      spoof." Reprinted: 1973.B40.

40   _____. "Textures of time." Manchester Guardian Weekly, 108
      (14 April), 25.
            Reprint of 1973.B39.

41   "PENDENNIS." "Amo Amis Amin Amat." The Observer, (11 Febru-
      ary), p. 44.
            A spoof on what books people read and Amis' answer.

42   PRESCOTT, PETER S. "Vintage Gumshoe." Newsweek, 82 (17 Sep-
      tember), 101-103.
            A Review of The Riverside Villas Murder. This is a skill-
      ful though tedious mystery, not up to a good novelist's stan-
      dards. It "moves slowly because Amis indulges himself in
      remembering period dance music and slang." Excerpted:
      1975.B11.

43 PRIAL, FRANK J. "Wine Talk: Warning About 'The Season': 'Tis
     Time of Eggnog Hangover." The New York Times (29 December),
     p. 18.
         Brief mention of On Drink with summary.

44 PRITCHETT, V.S. "Pugnacious Paradoxes." New Statesman, 85
     (19 January), 94-95.
         Brief mention of G.K. Chesterton: Selected Stories.
     Calls this a "frank and perceptive introduction." The ma-
     jority of the review concerns Chesterton.

45 QUINTON, ANTHONY. "Dancing to Troise's tune." London Evening
     Telegraph (8 April), p. 12.
         Brief favorable mention of The Riverside Villas Murder.

46 RICHARDSON, MAURICE. "Reader's Report." The Observer (8
     April), 37.
         Review of The Riverside Villas Murder. The novel is
     filled with contradictions, the character development
     clashes with the plot and detection, and the focus is dif-
     fused. The atmosphere and resolution are unconvincing.

47 RILEY, CAROLYN, ed. "Kingsley Amis," in Contemporary Literary
     Criticism: I. Detroit: Gale Research, pp. 5-6.
         Excerpts of 1963.B24; 1964.B2-B3; 1965.B22; 1967.B8;
     1971.B25.

48 SIGAL, CLANCY. "Band of Outlanders." National Review, 169
     (27 October), 25-26.
         On Drink is "funny, cynical, wise, entertaining, sensi-
     ble." Finds The Riverside Villas Murder enjoyable, and
     concludes that in Amis we see a rare virtue, for he refuses
     "to accept an imposed definition of what a Serious Writer
     ought to write about." Excerpted: 1975.B11.

49 STANFORD, DEREK. "poetry." Books & Bookmen, 18 (June), 106.
         Review of Tennyson, Selected by Kingsley Amis. "I have
     seen no neater assessment of Tennyson." Amis responds to
     the craftsman in Tennyson.

50 THWAITE, ANTHONY. "Japanese Lucky Jim." The Observer (4
     March), p. 37.
         Notes, in Natsumé Soseki's Botchan, a prefiguring of Jim
     Dixon by about 50 years.

51 TOYNBEE, PHILIP. "Pick of the Poets." The Observer (4 March),
     p. 37.
         Review of Tennyson, Selected by Kingsley Amis. Amis errs

1973

in assuming that Tennyson wrote virtually nothing of value
during the second half of his career. There is more to be
said about the writer than what Amis says.

52 TRACY, PHIL. Review of On Drink. The Village Voice (25 Sep-
    tember), pp. 34-35.
        Amis provides useful tips and affirms the wisdom of
    drink. Excerpted: 1975.B11.

53 VEIT, HENRI C. "Mystery, Detective and Suspense." Library
    Journal, 98 (1 September), 2466.
        Review of The Riverside Villas Murder. This is "more
    firmly planted in reality and more imaginative" than any
    1930's detective story he can recall. The trouble is tem-
    poral, for by forcing a point of view back to the 1930's,
    Amis' slang is too timely, the bands are mentioned by name
    too often, and the reminiscences of the Great War would al-
    ready be "old hat" in the 1930's.

54 WADE, ROSALIND. "Literary Supplement: Fiction Review." Con-
    temporary Review, 223 (July), 48.
        Review of The Riverside Villas Murder. Some might argue
    that the novel "wobbles between psychological-motivated por-
    trayals of some very off-beat characters and the standardised
    requirements of the conventional thriller," but this is of
    secondary importance. This is a "clever and original - doc-
    umented story."

55 WAUGH, AUBERON. "Auberon Waugh on the Mysteries of Hughes and
    Amis." The Spectator, 230 (14 April), 458-459.
        Review of The Riverside Villas Murder. An excellent nov-
    el, "part period pastiche, part parody, part original in-
    sight." Although Waugh admires the first half of the novel
    for its insights into childhood, he finds the murder story
    inept and preposterous. Concludes Amis "broods quietly and
    longingly about his own childhood."

56 WEALES, GERALD. Review of The Riverside Villas Murder. Hudson
    Review, 26 (Winter), 782.
        Except for Colonel Sun, this is Amis' "thinnest and mild-
    est" book to date. Although the early scenes are pleasant
    and diverting, the inept murder mystery that follows makes
    the reader wish Amis were parodying the genre. "Although
    Amis takes a light-hearted approach to the mystery novel,
    it is also an unmistakably sincere, almost loving one."

1974

*57   WHITE, JEAN M. "Mysteries." Book World, 7 (16 September), 6,
        10.
            Unlocatable. Listed incorrectly in 1976.A1.

58   WILSON, ANGUS. "A high talent flogging an old genre: The Riv-
        erside Villas Murder." The New York Times Book Review (11
        November), p. 6.
            The prose is pleasant in this "careful, loving recon-
        struction of the old genre." However, the improbable mech-
        anism behind the murder and the conventions of the 1930's
        detective story cramps Amis' artistry and creativity, re-
        sulting in "an oversimplified Edwardian view of human
        nature." Excerpted: 1975.B11.

1974 A BOOKS

1   SALWAK, DALE FRANCIS. "Kingsley Amis: Writer as Moralist."
        Ph. D. dissertation. University of Southern California.
            Since 1954--the year Lucky Jim was published--until 1973,
        when The Riverside Villas Murder was published--the devel-
        opment of Kingsley Amis' moral vision is clear and straight-
        forward. Beginning in a comic world filled with verbal
        jokes, comic masquerades and incidents, his view of life
        grows increasingly pessimistic until he arrives at a fear-
        fully grim vision of a nightmare world filled with hostility,
        violence, sexual abuse, and self-destruction. In his nov-
        els--as well as in his poetry--Amis stands for decency and
        common sense, for treating people rightly and honestly.
        His novels emphasize the necessity of good works, and of
        trying to live a moral life in the natural--as opposed to
        the supernatural--world.
            In addition to a study of Amis' writing career, the dis-
        sertation includes a selective bibliography listing primary
        and secondary sources, and the transcript of an interview
        the author conducted with Mr. Amis in 1973.

1974 B SHORTER WRITINGS

1   ACKROYD, PETER. "Clockwork Cuckoos." The Spectator, 232 (1
        June), p. 678.
            Review of Ending Up. Enjoys the "seedy realism" of the
        novel. Amis is saying, "Those who surrender to age are
        pathetic, and those who ignore it are laughable."

2   ANON. "Laughing at the aged." London Daily Express (30 May),
        p. 13.

1974

       Brief review of Ending Up. A new departure for Amis, as
he writes about a subject covered many times before, but
this time with new insights.

3   ANON. "Senile delinquents." The Times Literary Supplement
      (31 May), p. 575.
          Review of Ending Up. When Amis looks at life squarely
in this "farcical horror-story," fear results. Finds a
strong "sense of a man violently dreading what he must one
day become."

4   ANON. "Broken Down by Age and Sex." The Economist, 251 (8
      August), 106-107.
          Review of Ending Up. Amis doesn't preach on old age.
Rather, he studies behavior and resources in a blend of humor and wounding realism.

5   ANON. "PW Forecasts: Ending Up." Publishers' Weekly, 206
      (12 August), 50.
          Amis is at his "most perverse and entertaining" in a nov-
el which is "as perfectly seasoned with black humor as it
is consistent with his characters' psychology."

6   BREEN, JON L. "The World of Mysteries." Wilson Library Bul-
      letin, 48 (February), 465.
          Cites The Riverside Villas Murder as best novel of the
year, noting that the characters are more memorable than
the crime.

7   BROYARD, ANATOLE. "Good-by to the Benign." The New York
      Times (5 October), p. 29.
          Review of Ending Up. The novel is "a savage and rela-
tively humorless attack on its five characters, leaving the
reader to wonder why the author created them if he finds
them so stunted and irredeemable." Moreover, the novel
"ends in such a brutal and pointless apocalypse that it is
difficult to avoid psychoanalytic speculations about the
source of Mr. Amis's animosity."

8   CARRINGTON, C.E. "Broken down by age and sex." The Economist,
      247 (8 June), 106-107.
          Review of Ending Up. The novel recalls Muriel Spark's
Memento Mori and William Trevor's The Old Boys. Amis
doesn't lecture on the problems of old age, but concentrates
on the behavior and resources of five characters, all living
on borrowed time, bound by weakness and "a bored malice."
Amis writes about them "with a precise savagery that is both
funny and deeply wounding."

9   COOK, BRUCE. "Bernard Hates Everybody: Laughter and Truth
    Mingle in Ending Up." The National Observer (9 November),
    p. 25.
        "If literature has a higher purpose...it must be to ease
    the burden of the human condition." Amis does not do this
    in Ending Up, a novel which "contains more mean laughs and
    uncomfortable truths per page than any book since Waugh's
    Handful of Dust."

10 COYNE, PATRICIA S. "Books in Brief." National Review, 26 (1
    February), 153.
        Review of The Riverside Villas Murder. Although this is
    a "shoddy vehicle" unsatisfying in detection, Amis' second-
    ary characters, style, and dialogue are eminently satisfying.
    Excerpted: 1975.B11.

11 DOYLE, PAUL A. "Fiction." Best Sellers, 34 (15 October), 320.
        Review of Ending Up. Except for Lucky Jim, Amis really
    hasn't said anything in his fiction. Notes a "moral flab-
    biness or an amoral flabbiness" about Amis and his writing.
    Also, he lacks the "solidity" most satirists and many hu-
    morists possess. He also lacks "genuine substance" or a
    serious philosophical commitment in his writings.

12 EGREMONT, MAX. "Growing old disgracefully." Books & Bookmen,
    19 (June), 92.
        Review of Ending Up. A skillfully written novel which
    presents "old age in all its horror and its helplessness."

13 ELLIOTT, JANICE. "Out with A Bang." London Sunday Telegraph
    (2 June), p. 15.
        Brief mention of Ending Up.

14 FOOTE, TIMOTHY. "Geriatricks." Time, 104 (30 September), 93.
        Review of Ending Up. In Amis' later novels, there is a
    spreading "swinishness" of character and a distaste Amis
    seems to feel for his creations. In his latest novel, he
    is a merciless misanthrope. This is a "mean microcosm" of
    Little England.

15 HEALD, TIM. "Recent Fiction." London Daily Telegraph (31
    May), p. 40.
        Brief mention of Ending Up. Amis' characters are dis-
    tinct and his plotting is skillful.

16 HIGGINS, JOHN. "Critic's Choice: The Times reviewers select
    their books of 1974." London Times (28 November), p. iv.
        Cites Ending Up as book of the year. Amis' sharp eye

1974

for the dislikable monsters here even makes "middle age look dangerous, which I suspect was one of Mr. Amis's intentions."

17   JAMES, CLIVE.   "Books of the Year."   The Observer (15 December), p. 19.
      Cites Ending Up as book of the year, calling it "one of his most interesting."

18   _____.   "Profile 4: Kingsley Amis."   New Review, 1 (July), 21-28.
      Interview in which Amis comments on the processes and problems of writing. Covers most of his works up to 1974.

19   KENNEDY, ALAN. "Conclusion: A Quick Look Around," in his The Protean Self: Dramatic Action in Contemporary Fiction. New York: Columbia University Press, pp. 269-272.
      The humor in Lucky Jim results from what Dixon wishes he could do and what he actually says. He turns to a private means of self-dramatization but obeys what convention demands of the situation. This becomes comic. "His attempts at private drama are not then, we are told, valid attempts at ritual self-expression. They are neurotic denials of freedom, and in fact merely an inverted form of imprisonment to his situation."

20   KINSMAN, CLARE D. and MARY ANN TENNENHOUSE, eds. "Kingsley Amis," in Contemporary Authors: A Bibliographic Guide to Current Authors and Their Works. Detroit: Gale, p. 47.
      Brief critical study with short bibliography of primary and secondary sources.

21   LEVIN, BERNARD. "Books of the Year." The Observer (15 December), p. 19.
      Cites Ending Up as book of the year, calling it a "brilliant, honest, brutal, haunting book."

22   LODGE, DAVID. "Comic yet serious." Tablet, 228 (29 June), 626.
      Review of Ending Up. Ever since Take A Girl Like You, Amis' novels "have usually been spoiled by a certain meretriciousness or laziness or self-indulgence at crucial points." This is not so in Ending Up, "a black-comic novella about old age and death." Unlike Muriel Spark's Memento Mori, there is no hint of transcendence, the supernatural, in the world; "hence the peculiar bleakness of its images of mortality." This is certainly Amis' best novel in years: "comic yet wholly serious, compassionate without being sentimental."

23 M., J. "How To Stump A Developer!" London Evening News (1
    June), p. 23.
        Brief review of Ending Up with a summary of its plot and
    characters.

24 MARSHMENT, MARGARET. "Racism for Fun." Joliso, 2 (February),
    61-68.
        Discussion of The James Bond Dossier with summary of its
    contents.

25 MELLORS, JOHN. "A Piano Tuner's Son: the Novels of Kingsley
    Amis." The London Magazine, NS 14 (August-September), 102-
    106.
        Examines Amis' novels through Ending Up and concludes
    that his funniest novel, Lucky Jim, is so successful because
    of its skillful design and fast action, mimicry, style, and
    attitude to life (hatred of phonies). Moreover, every comic
    situation has in it the seeds of more, and this, together
    with the broad comedy theme of the put-upon hero who turns
    the tables, makes it an especially appealing novel. Says
    the story sags in Ending Up.

26 MOON, ERIC. "Fiction." Library Journal, 99 (1 October), 2498.
        Review of Ending Up. The novel "speaks the desperation
    of a writer who knows he's lost his talent....Almost unprec-
    edented for bad taste and sick humor, this novel is boring
    when it is not disgusting in its cynicism and exploitation."

27 ORAM, MALCOLM. "PW Interviews: Kingsley Amis." Publishers'
    Weekly, 206 (28 October), 6-7.
        Interview with Amis covering his childhood, his tech-
    nique as a writer, and his belief in maintaining a wide
    range. Says he is never autobiographical in his fiction.
    Lucky Jim is about boredom and the power of the bores.

28 PETERS, PAULINE. "Two on an island." London Sunday Times
    Magazine (3 February), pp. 64-66.
        Profile on Amis and his wife, including details on their
    family background, house, finances and marriage.

29 PRESCOTT, PETER S. "Mates and Inmates." Newsweek, 84 (30 Sep-
    tember), 103.
        Review on Ending Up. Amis has a sharp eye for detail
    "in depicting the wretchedness or deterioration of man and
    his effects." Amis' satirical skill seems wasted, however,
    for there is "no sense of dread, no horror of the flesh."
    By the end, the author seems bored.

1974

30 PRINCE, PETER. "Euthanasia." New Statesman, 87 (31 May), 776.
        Review of Ending Up. In this study of the stigma of
    being old, Amis shows that age affects all they do, think,
    and say, "so that all their rages lose force and dwindle
    into farcical spites, and all their joys are perilously en-
    tertained." Concludes that the ending is too hurried.

31 RABAN, JONATHAN. "What Shall We Do about Anthony Burgess?"
    Encounter, 43 (November), 87-88.
        Review of Ending Up. The characters come alive in this
    "brutal comedy which is not so much about old age as about
    the problem of why people even bother to get born at all."
    However, Amis' pessimism is overwhelmed by the force of his
    good humor.

32 RATCLIFFE, MICHAEL. "Bleak house." London Times (30 May),
    p. 10.
        Review of Ending Up. This is the most bleak and unfor-
    giving of anything Amis has written, but not hateful in the
    manner of One Fat Englishman because it is written from a
    "cool disgust" that life should come to this. Although
    some brief moments of compassion lighten this mood a little,
    Amis refrains from diagnosis and prescription, giving the
    book an unfocused center. Amis proceeds with uncertainty,
    for his figures are without two-dimensional comic life of
    their own, and Amis never says what he actually wants to
    say about old age.

33 RILEY, CAROLYN and BARBARA HARTE, eds. "Kingsley Amis," in
    Contemporary Literary Criticism: II. Detroit: Gale, pp.
    4-11.
        Excerpts of 1962.B12; 1963.B23; 1964.B11; 1966.B10, B13,
    B48; 1967.B5, B19; 1968.B12-B13, B52, B54; 1969.B28, B36,
    B41; 1970.B7, B9, B21, B25, B29, B38; 1971.B24; 1972.B20.

34 SALE, ROGER. "Fooling Around, and Serious Business." The
    Hudson Review, 27 (Winter), 626-627.
        Review of Ending Up. Amis is "frightened of life...and
    possessed by death." This is a waste of his talent because
    he hasn't faced up to his fear and made it the center of
    his books. Says the characters exist only so Amis "can
    wound them."

35 SIGAL, CLANCY. "Recent, Notable Fiction." New Republic, 171
    (12 October), 27-28.
        Review of Ending Up. From Lucky Jim on, Amis' heroes
    resemble Billy Bunter. Amis' compassion tempers his basic

sourness in this "cruel, upsetting and at times extremely funny" novel. The book is both serious and funny, and helps to exorcise some fears of old age. Despite the horrors of being old, he seems to be saying, one can still be "triumphantly human." Excerpted: 1976.B20.

36   SISSMAN, L.E. "Books: Miss, Near Miss, Hit." The New Yorker, 50 (21 October), 185.
        Brief review of Ending Up. A funny and tender book, spoiled by its "mechanistic structure" and forced ending. Excerpted: 1976.B20.

37   SMITH, GODFREY. "Amis at his best." London Sunday Times (2 June), p. 40.
        Review of Ending Up. "The linguistic skills which can dramatise in four lines of dialogue a lifetime's mutual loathing, the visual imagery,...the uncanny feel for life as it is actually being lived are all deployed as Amis stretches himself to the full limit of his formidable powers." The characters are fully realized: "flesh and blood, three-dimensional, human, fallible, all too mortal, and as comic as they are tragic." Criticizes Amis for too many excretory jokes and the over-wrought ending, somewhat reminiscent of the stage at the end of Hamlet. Also, the characters would have been more credible if ten years older.

38   STADE, GEORGE. "A Spark, an Amis, a Rhys." The New York Times Book Review (20 October), p. 5.
        Review of Ending Up. Like Lucky Jim and The Green Man, Amis makes the most of his virtues and limitations in Ending Up. The characters seem all too human; the story is "funny and upsetting, but not tendentious."

39   TOYNBEE, PHILIP. "Kicking the bucket." The Observer (2 June), p. 33.
        Review of Ending Up. Like Burgess' Enderby's End, Amis' novel is a tragic-comic study of the aged. But there the similarities end. Amis' style is honed, shaved, and clarified (like Compton-Burnett's), whereas Burgess always enjoys elaborations. Moreover, Ending Up is both funny and serious. Amis shows us real people and real suffering. He has risen above satire with no axe to grind. The book "is full of dread before the spectacle of old age, the appalling threat of senility." But Amis doesn't rant against old age; rather, he witnesses it, is awed by it, and manages, in his own way, to master it."

1974

40   TREVOR, WILLIAM. "Unhappy ending." Manchester Guardian (30
     May), p. 11.
          Review of Ending Up. Although Amis skillfully draws the
     reader into his world, one can't help wishing he had devel-
     oped it further, for as it stands the novel is little more
     than a long short story. The ending is "bald and
     unconvincing."

41   VAIZEY, JOHN. "Compliments of the Season." The Listener, 91
     (30 May), 703-704.
          Review of Ending Up. To his "classically pure,...exactly
     and accurately idiomatic" English, Amis has added a new
     depth of human feeling unseen in the earlier novels. This
     book is much like a film script or radio play in the way
     Amis has linked the episodes together. Some of the jokes
     arise from familiar Amis situations. Excerpted: 1976.B20.

42   WADE, ROSALIND. "Literary Supplement: Q. Fiction Review."
     Contemporary Review, 225 (July), 47.
          Review of Ending Up. Amis doesn't gloss over a depres-
     sing, unattractive situation nor do his characters engage
     in self-pity. Instead, they try to derive as much satis-
     faction from their circumstances as possible. Says the
     ending strains credulity too far, however.

43   WAUGH, AUBERON. "It may seem funny." London Evening Standard
     (11 June), p. 25.
          Brief review of Ending Up. Though funny on the surface,
     Amis is deadly serious as he comments on aging and the
     afflictions of the aged.

1975 A BOOKS

1   GOHN, JACK BENOIT. "The Novels of Kingsley Amis: A Reading."
    Ph. D. dissertation, Johns Hopkins University.
         A detailed analysis of Amis' novels for theme, structure,
    and development.

2   KELLY, THOMAS LEE. "The Quest for Self in the Early Novels of
    Kingsley Amis." Pd. D. dissertation, The University of
    Oklahoma.
         Examines Amis' first five novels to illustrate his chang-
    ing view of man's quest for self-discovery in the modern
    world. This quest provides a structural and thematic basis
    for the novels. Follows the quest pattern in Joseph
    Campbell's The Hero with A Thousand Faces.

1975 B SHORTER WRITINGS

1   ANON. "Language and Literature." Choice, 12 (May), 387-388.
        Review of Ending Up. As a "comic delight and a sardonic
     comment on the incongruities, injustices, and indignities
     of life, which aging only intensifies," this is one of Amis'
     best. It reminds one of Iris Murdoch's fiction in tone and
     technique. "More concerned with the interaction of the
     characters in the group than with the one alienated outsider
     we so often find in his work."

2   ANON. "The Novelist as Provocateur." New Statesman, 87 (14
     February), 202-203.
        Sees early signs of Amis' conversion to Conservatism in
     his education as a youth and at St. John's College, Oxford.

3   BOULTON, MARJORIE. The Anatomy of the Novel. London and
     Boston: Routledge and Kegan Paul, pp. 21-98, passim.
        In Take A Girl Like You, Amis switches between two points
     of view so the reader can watch Jenny and Patrick's pathet-
     ically inadequate relationship develop. This is far more
     effective than moralizing. Amis is able to show the reader
     how far apart the two really are, from one another and from
     deep love.

4   BRAGG, MELVYN. "Kingsley Amis looks back--an interview with
     Melvyn Bragg." The Listener, 93 (20 February), 240-241.
        Amis comments on his education, Lucky Jim, American writ-
     ers, sex, themes in his writings, and politics.

5   GUREWITCH, MORTON. "The Imagination of Farce," in his Comedy:
     The Irrational Vision. Ithaca and London: Cornell Univer-
     sity Press, pp. 158-159.
        Jim Dixon exemplifies "psychic farce"; that is, "he
     manages a happy avoidance of certifiable mental imbalance."
     He preserves his sanity via fantasies, mimicry, and bodily
     contortions.

6   HODGART, MATTHEW. "Time Trips." The New York Review of Books
     (20 March), p. 32.
        Review of Ending Up. Apparently, "we are to read the
     book not as a realistic chronicle or a picture of life as
     lived in Britain today, but rather as some kind of fable."
     Suggests that Amis has modeled the novel's structure on a
     baroque suite or a classical work with some movements in
     sonata form, possibly Mozart's g minor. Sees a symmetry in
     horribleness of all five characters and in virtuousness
     of all five, as well as in a balance of pleasure and pain.

1975

> This gives the novel a balance in form. In effect, Amis is
> trying to give some formal pattern "to the futility and mean-
> inglessness of life as it appears to old people." Excerpted:
> 1976.B20.

7   HOLLOWAY, DAVID. "The Amis Family." London <u>Daily Telegraph</u>
(9 August), pp. 10, 11.
> Biographical article covering the backgrounds, writing
> habits, and related interests of wife Elizabeth Janeway,
> son Martin, and Kingsley Amis himself.

8   JONES, D.A.N. "Sweet and boyish master." <u>The Listener</u>, 94
(25 December), 890.
> Review of <u>Rudyard Kipling and His World</u>. Some of the
> pictures contradict or counterpoint Amis, who keeps sex,
> religion and politics to a minimum.

9   MASON, PHILIP. "Philip Mason on Amis, Kipling and the Modern
Mind." <u>The Spectator</u>, 233 (15 November), 634.
> Review of <u>Rudyard Kipling and His World</u>. Says he is far
> more surprised by what Amis doesn't say than by what he does
> say. Wishes Amis had explored the reasons for some people
> identifying with Kipling and others disliking him. Disagrees
> with Amis' contention that Kipling's work was minimally af-
> fected by his life.

10   NICOL, CHARLES. "A Brittle Pencil." <u>National Review</u>, 27 (14
March), 296-297.
> Brief review of <u>Ending Up</u>. Because of the unconvincing,
> thin characters, reading <u>Ending Up</u> "is like watching a clock
> run down." After we've seen the characters, there's little
> more to do. "Although all the characters are drawn with a
> fine, sharp, brittle pencil, there is little shading in
> their paper thin personalities." Excerpted: 1976.B20.

11   RILEY, CAROLYN, ed. "Kingsley Amis," in <u>Contemporary Literary
Criticism: IV</u>. Detroit: Gale Research, pp. 7-10.
> Excerpts of 1971.B2; 1973.B7, B27, B34, B42, B48, B52,
> B59; 1974.B11, B56; 1975.B13.

12   SALWAK, DALE. "An Interview with Kingsley Amis." <u>Contemporary
Literature</u>, 16 (Winter), 1-18.
> Covers <u>Lucky Jim</u> through <u>The Riverside Villas Murder</u>,
> with Amis commenting on their substance and morality, along
> with the literary establishment in England, the "Angry Young
> Men," the political novel, his childhood and poetry.

13   SPACKS, PATRICIA MEYER. "New Novels: In the Dumps." The Yale
      Review, 64 (Summer), 585-587.
           Review of Ending Up. A grotesque comedy in which Amis
      tries to make comedy of images of depression and the horrors
      of old age. The tone is uneasy, but Amis plausibly pene-
      trates the anger and frustration of these people. "The ob-
      sessive narrowness of vision" makes the tone not quite
      trustworthy. Excerpted: 1976.B20.

14   THEROUX PAUL. "Ruddy." New Statesman, 90 (21 November), 648.
           Review of Rudyard Kipling and His World. Amis "is nei-
      ther haunted nor unsettled by a man he quietly acknowledges
      to be an imperialist, a racialist, and a paternalist." But
      there is nothing new to the study; rather, the purpose of
      Amis is to examine and reinterpret details already in
      existence.

1976 A BOOKS

1   GOHN, JACK BENOIT. Kingsley Amis: A Checklist. Series #34.
      Kent: Kent State University Press, 167 pp.
           Covers primary and secondary materials through 1975 with
      occasional annotations. Secondary items are divided into
      two sections: materials of critical, biographical and bib-
      liographical interest in the first, and reviews in the
      second.

1976 B SHORTER WRITINGS

1   ANON. "Announcements." Kirkus, 44 (15 January), 122.
           Brief mention of Rudyard Kipling and His World.

2   ANON. "Briefly Noted." The New Yorker, 52 (8 March), 131.
           Brief mention of Rudyard Kipling and His World. Despite
      Amis' diligent efforts, Kipling remains "as strange, as
      withdrawn, and as mysterious as ever."

3   ANON. "Biography." Library Journal, 101 (15 March), 805.
           Brief mention of Rudyard Kipling and His World. The
      study is too objective and marred by Amis' defense of the
      "white man's burden."

4   ANON. "Literation." Booklist, 72 (1 June), 1234.
           Brief mention of Rudyard Kilping and His World. Amis
      skims the highlights of Kipling. A good introductory book.

1976

5   ANON. "Recent fiction: Out of the frying pan." The Economist,
     261 (16 October), 143.
          Review of The Alteration. Calls this a mordant "parable
     upon the nature of tyranny, of individual and institutional
     self-love, of man's catastrophic inability to love his neigh-
     bor." Reflects Anthony Burgess' "themes of music, Catholi-
     cism, the conflict of Pelagian and Augustinian modes in the
     English character."

6   ANON. "Fiction." Kirkus, 44 (15 November), 1233.
          Review of The Alteration. Missing in this "gimmicky,
     half-parodied, sentimental melodrama" is Amis' light touch
     and high spirits. Says it has a "deus ex machina denouement,
     and an ironic, downbeat epilogue."

7   BANNON, BARBARA A. "PW Forecasts: Fiction." Publishers'
     Weekly, 209 (16 February), 92.
          Brief mention of paperback reprint of Ending Up.

8   BAYLEY, JOHN. "Paleface." The New York Review of Books (15
     April), pp. 30-32.
          Review of Rudyard Kipling and His World. Like Philip
     Mason's Kipling: The Glass, the Shadow and the Fire, Amis'
     study tells the known facts about Kipling with "sense and
     shrewdness, avoiding speculation" and quite prepared not to
     question anything other than the work left behind.

9   BELL, PEARL K. "Letter from London." New Leader, 59 (6 De-
     cember), 4.
          Review of The Alteration. This is "a sly historical
     fiction" that could also be read as "a kind of social-sci-
     ence fiction." It is, however, too tricky and inconsequen-
     tial, and its satiric irony is diminished "by his capricious
     and uninspired, fooling around."

10   CAREY, JOHN. "IF." New Statesman, 92 (8 October), 483.
          Review of The Alteration. This is a study of tyranny.
     "By showing what a horrible notion world government is, Amis
     usefully corrects the tendency to regard it as a panacea."
     The boy's predicament is integral to the book, "since the
     emasculation of life and art is its major theme." Says
     Amis carefully conveys Hubert's bewilderment and feelingly
     traces the pain in other minds.

11   COSGRAVE, MARY SILVA. "Outlook Tower." Horn Book Magazine,
     52 (December), 651.
          Brief review of Rudyard Kipling and His World. Amis sees

Kipling's life as less controversial and his work as more
outstanding than did earlier critics. Offers personal,
terse comments on Kipling's successes and failures.

12   GLEASON, W.F. "Fiction." Best Sellers, 36 (May), p. 45.
        Brief favorable mention of The Alteration. Includes a
plot summary and comments on the "grimness" of the story.

13   GREEN, MARTIN. "Amis and Drabble look back." The New York
        Times Book Review (18 April), pp. 6, 14.
        Review of Rudyard Kipling and His World. "A fresh and
original reflection on the subject." Reveals Amis' conser-
vatism. The clear, straightforward style matches his old-
fashioned opinions.

14   IRWIN, MICHAEL. "The unkindest cut of all." The Times Literary
        Supplement (8 October), p. 1269.
        Review of The Alteration. In That Uncertain Feeling, One
Fat Englishman, and The Green Man, Amis has difficulty ad-
justing his gifts for comedy to the things he wants to say,
often serious. In Ending Up, "the gap between comic means
and serious ends has widened." The Alteration, however, is
far beyond Amis' earlier range. It is a deadly serious work
in a fantastical context. The threat to Hubert is the "manifestation of a pervasive evil." Despite its strengths, however, the narrative level is uncertain and the numerous
transcription jokes distract the reader.

15   JAMES, CLIVE. "Books of the Year." The Observer (12 December),
        p. 26.
        Cites The Alteration as book of the year.

16   JOHNSON, PAMELA HANSFORD. "In Father Bond's day." The Lis-
        tener, 97 (7 October), 453.
        Review of The Alteration. It is necessary to keep in
mind that this is a 1976 book, "or the book may begin to
read like a costume drama." It may be read just for enjoyment, or as a basically serious and scholarly work with
overtones of Dostoevsky in the interview between the Friar,
Flackerty and Lyall. Calls this a triumph of rapid switch
of mood, "from felicity to black apprehension, from 'bad'
taste to good."

17   LARKIN, PHILIP. "Books of the Year." The Observer (12 De-
        cember), p. 26.
        Cites The Alteration as book of the year. Amis "has
never been more audaciously imaginative" in this "doubly
extraordinary novel."

1976

18   LOWENKRON, DAVID HENRY. "Glimpses of Another World." <u>South-
     west Review</u>, 61 (Autumn), 435-438.
         Review of <u>Rudyard Kipling and His World</u>. Although there's
     nothing new in this study, Amis does succeed in correcting
     the viewpoint about Kipling by reminding us that his art
     transcends his politics. The book also reveals that Amis
     has been wooed by the establishment. "Never having had a
     consistent set of values, he finds it easy to become an apol-
     ogist for his old antagonist."

19   NYE, ROBERT. Review of <u>The Alteration</u>. <u>Christian Science
     Monitor</u> (31 March), p. 19.
         A valuable book representing the point of view of a nov-
     elist of a different time, mood and style. Amis stays
     closely to the text.

20   RILEY, CAROLYN and PHYLLIS CARMEL MENDELSON, eds. "Kingsley
     Amis," in <u>Contemporary Literary Criticism: V</u>. Detroit:
     Gale Research, pp. 20-24.
         Excerpts of: 1967.B28 (<u>see also</u> 1966.B51); 1974.B34-B36,
     B42; 1975.B6, B10, B13.

21   SEYMOUR-SMITH, MARTIN. "Kingsley Amis," in his <u>Who's Who in
     Twentieth Century Literature</u>. New York: Holt, Rinehart
     and Winston, p. 23.
         Brief mention of Amis. Includes biographical background
     and comments on the thematic contents of his novels through
     <u>The Riverside Villas Murder</u>.

22   SMALL, CHRISTOPHER. "Images of Kipling." <u>Sewanee Review</u>, 84
     (July), 490.
         Brief review of <u>Rudyard Kipling and His World</u>. Amis shows
     ambiguities between deference to a great writer and the
     faults he finds.

23   TOTTON, NICK. "Diminuendo." <u>The Spectator</u>, 237 (9 October),
     22.
         Review of <u>The Alteration</u>. Although there's much fun,
     Amis doesn't handle his subject adroitly in this science
     fiction novel. Hubert Anvil is too resourceful to be cred-
     ible. His sexual latency isn't believable. The other char-
     acters are also cardboard. The plot is trivial, and the
     conclusion is coincidental.

24   TOYNBEE, PHILIP. "The Pope's gelding." <u>The Observer</u> (10 Oc-
     tober), p. 27.
         Review of <u>The Alteration</u>. Praises Amis' unpredictability
     in this combination satire, fantasy, adventure story, science

fiction tale and genuine tragedy. In this plausible novel, the decencies "are almost all with the rebels; and even now the notion of a Roman Church restored to the fullness of its power is enough to make any libertarian shudder."

1977 A BOOKS - NONE

1977 B SHORTER WRITINGS

1   ADAMS, P.L. Review of The Alteration. Atlantic Monthly, 239 (February), 98.
    The grim story and fanciful setting never blend. "As an attack on corrupt, tyrannical government it seems needlessly oblique, while as anticlericalism it comes some centuries late."

2   ANON. "fiction." Booklist, 73 (1 January), 650.
    Review of The Alteration. The plot serves as "backdrop for Amis's wild extrapolations as he wrenches historical chronology askew."

3   ANON. "Briefly Noted." The New Yorker, 53 (14 March), 138.
    Review of The Alteration. Amis "is at his most amusing, his most ironic, and his most exhilarating." He shows contemporary England as it might have been had the Reformation not occurred, if Luther had become Pope, and if the Roman Catholic Church controlled all Christendom.

4   CLEMONS, WALTER. "Now and Never-Never." Newsweek, 89 (17 January), 84.
    Review of The Alteration. The first half of this book is much better; the latter half--escape, abduction, rescue-- is a boy's adventure and might be a rewrite of Treasure Island.

5   COOK, BRUCE. "Autumn Anger." Saturday Review, 4 (5 February), 28-29.
    Review of The Alteration. This is the most theological of Amis' books; it fits into the pattern of a developing metaphysical concern first seen in The Anti-Death League. Amis vents his anger against the Catholic faith, the Catholic idea of God, and "the big lie," Christianity. "It is an almost bitter book by a man grown angry in middle age."

6   DAVIS, L.J. "Hey, Everyone, How're We Doing?" The National Observer (29 January), p. 21.
    Review of The Alteration. This novel will probably get

1977

more serious attention than it deserves. Amis is having fun and is playing "an intellectual game entered into with imagination and zest." In the United States this element of play is almost unknown.

7   EDWARDS, THOMAS R. "Getting Away from It All." The New York Review of Books (3 March), p. 31.
       Review of The Alteration. The major premise to Amis' kind of novels is "the stimulating variety of detail in a story of crime or imagined worlds leads finally back to an idea of human nature as immutably fixed and gravely flawed." In The Alteration, Amis catches Hubert's puzzlement over castration to develop the theme, "Whatever is, is--if not right, at least tolerable and probably no worse than anything else."

8   FORREST, ALAN. "A year's good reading." Books & Bookmen, 22 (January), 57.
       Brief mention of The Alteration. A new excursion into science fiction with "some splendid moments."

9   GRAY, PAUL. "Blood of the Lamb." Time, 109 (3 January), 81-82.
       Review of The Alteration. Hubert's struggle is set against a background of "intriguing conjectures and sly jokes," as Amis combines satire, science fiction, boys' adventure and travelogue.

10   LEHMANN-HAUPT, CHRISTOPHER. "Books of The Times." The New York Times (14 January), p. C19.
       Review of The Alteration. The novel's premise and plot are especially enjoyable and absorbing, but Lehmann-Haupt doubts they go together. Comments on the beautiful prose, the clockwork plot, and the satire, which seems to be saying it would have been a catastrophe if the Reformation hadn't occurred. Is troubled because the implications about castration are never resolved. Unable to tell what Amis meant by the ending.

11   NELSON, MILO G. "fiction." Library Journal, 102 (1 April), 830.
       Brief review of The Alteration. A serio-comic fantasy with a hazy moral lesson and not much to admire in spite of the elaborately structured plot.

12   O'HARA, J.D. "what if Luther had been Pope." The New York Times Book Review (30 January), pp. 4, 27.
       Review of The Alteration. In this science fiction novel,

Amis' strength is in "the tangential humor" and his weakness is in simple characters and a melodramatic plot. The
ending is absurdly disappointing.

13 REEDY, GERARD C. "Fiction." America, 136 (7 May), 422-423.
        Brief review of The Alteration. Although Amis tries to
    be profound in this depiction of "ecclesiastical hypocrisy,"
    the novel is "more funny than profound."

14 SWANSON, DONALD R. "books." Antioch Review, 35 (Winter), 122.
        Review of Rudyard Kipling and His World. In this picture
    book with accompanying biographical-critical essay, Amis
    creates a living character. The study is like a well-plotted
    novel.

Index

The following index is arranged alphabetically in one sequence. Except for very brief mentions, it includes all of the authors, titles, and subjects of works listed in this bibliography. The index also includes a number of specialized subject headings under the main heading of "Kingsley Amis": bibliography, biography, interview. Index references are to item numbers. To find a specific item, turn to the date, section ("A" for books, "B" for shorter writings), and number listed.

"Amis is Thrilled About Thrillers," 1968.B6
"Amis is Writing James Bond
Book," 1967.B24
Amis, Kingsley
--Bibliography, 1963.B24;
1966.B60; 1967.B7, B15;
1969.B18, B45; 1970.B1, B24;
1973.B47; 1974.A1, B20;
1976.A1
--Biography, 1955.B10; 1957.B26;
1958.B13-14, B45; 1959.B9;
1962.B4, B35; 1963.B24;
1964.B7, B25; 1965.B2;
1967.B9, B11, B12; 1969.B9,
B18, B42; 1970.B24; 1972.B24;
1975.B2, B4, B7, B12;
1976.B21
--Interview, 1955.B10; 1958.B5;
1960.B32; 1961.B45; 1962.B15,
B30-31; 1965.B38; 1967.B2,
B24, B31; 1968.B2, B10, B17;
1970.B13; 1974.B18, B27;
1975.B4, B12
"Amis, McCarthy, Naipaul,"
1972.B36
"Amis: nostalgia for the
thirties," 1973.B19
"Amis on Bond," 1965.B37
"Amis on Fleming: it takes
40,000 critical words,"
1968.B62
"Amis View of Bond, The,"
1967.B13
Amory, Cleveland, 1968.B3
"Amusing Story of Life at a Pro-
vincial University," 1954.B7
"Analysis of the Novels of
Kingsley Amis, An," 1965.A1
"Androids All," 1961.B19
"Angries: Is There a Protestant
in the House, The," 1962.B18
"Angry Englishman," 1964.B9
"Angry Young Man Revisited, The,"
1965.B46
"Angry Young Men," 1958.B9
Anon., 1951.B1; 1954.B2-6;
1955.B1; 1956.B3; 1957.B1-4;
1958.B4-8; 1960.B3-4, B6-9;
1961.B1-4, B6-7; 1962.B1-2,
B4; 1963.B1-4; 1964.B5-7;

1965.B2-3, B5-15; 1966.B1-9;
1967.B2-4; 1968.B5-7, B9-10;
1969.B3-4; 1970.B1, B3-4;
1971.B2; 1972.B3, B6-7, B11-
12; 1973.B3-17, 1974.B2-3;
1975.B1-2; 1976.B5-6;
1977.B2-3
Anti-Death League, The, 1966.B3,
B5-11, B14-16, B19-23, B26,
B29-30, B32, B37-39, B41, B43,
B47-48, B52-53, B55, B57-58,
B62, B64-66; 1967.B3, B10;
1968.B37, B56; 1969.B33, B38,
B41; 1970.B7-9, B12; 1972.B17,
B48; 1974.A1; 1975.B12
"Anti-Heel and Non Heiress,"
1969.B14
"Anti-Heroides," 1955.B8
"Anti-Intellectual Intellectualism
in the Postwar English Novel,"
1971.B41
"Anything Goes," 1966.B10
"Appetite for Booze and Helene,
An," 1964.B12
"Appleyard among the millionaires,"
1968.B32
"Art of Bungling," 1958.B2
"As Read in London," 1958.B27
"Auberon Waugh on the Mysteries
of Hughes and Amis," 1973.B55
"Autumn Anger," 1977.B5
"Away from this Body," 1969.B10
"Awful Mr. Micheldene and Other
Monsters," 1964.B32

"Bacchus and pards," 1972.B49
"Back to the bad old days,"
1964.B33
"Bad Conscience," 1955.B7
Bailhache, Jean, 1958.B9
Baker, Roger, 1968.B11
Balakian, Nona, 1959.B2
Ball, Patricia, 1962.B5
"Band of Outlanders," 1973.B48
Barrett, William, 1964.B9
"Beastly Business," 1964.B5
"Beastly to God," 1966.B3
Beavan, John, 1957.B5
"Beginning with Amis," 1955.B20
Bell, Pearl K., 1970.B6; 1971.B4;
1976.B9

DATE DUE

FEB 0 3 1995		
FEB 2 1 1995		
GAYLORD		PRINTED IN U.S.A.